Contents

Chapter 1: Introduction to Ruby on Rails..21

1.1 What is Ruby on Rails?...21

History of Ruby on Rails..21

Key Features of Ruby on Rails...21

Setting Up Your Development Environment...22

Hello World in Rails..22

The MVC Architecture in Rails..23

1.2 A Brief History of Ruby on Rails...23

Birth of Ruby on Rails...23

Release of Ruby on Rails 1.0...24

The Rise of the Rails Community...24

The Rails Doctrine and Philosophy...24

Major Versions and Improvements..24

The Continuing Evolution..25

1.3 Setting Up Your Development Environment..25

1.3.1 Installing Ruby...25

1.3.2 Installing Rails...26

1.3.3 Database Setup..27

1.3.4 Text Editor or IDE..27

1.3.5 Version Control..27

1.3.6 Web Server..27

Conclusion..28

1.4 Hello World in Rails...28

Creating a New Rails Project..28

Exploring the Project Structure...28

Generating a Controller and View...29

Editing the View...29

Starting the Rails Server...29

Understanding the Route..29

Conclusion..30

1.5 The MVC Architecture in Rails...30

Understanding MVC..30

How MVC Works in Rails...30

Routing in Rails 31

Benefits of MVC in Rails...32

Chapter 2: Getting Started with Ruby 33

2.1 Understanding Ruby Syntax..33

Variables and Data Types..33

Control Flow and Loops...33

Strings and String Interpolation 34

Symbols...34

Comments..35

Conclusion 35

2.2 Variables and Data Types..35

Variable Assignment..35

Data Types in Ruby 35

Type Conversion 36

Strings and String Manipulation 36

Symbols...36

Constants...36

Conclusion 37

2.3 Control Flow and Loops 37

Conditional Statements..37

Loops..38

Iterators 38

Breaking and Exiting Loops 39

Conclusion 39

2.4 Arrays and Hashes in Ruby...39

Arrays 39

Hashes 40

Iterating through Arrays and Hashes 40

Conclusion 41

2.5 Ruby Methods and Functions 41

Defining Methods..41

Calling Methods..41

Method Parameters 41

Default Values for Parameters 42

Returning Values 42

Scope of Variables 42

Conclusion 42

Chapter 3: Building Your First Rails Application 43

3.1 Creating a New Rails Project 43

Prerequisites 43

Creating a New Rails Project 43

Project Structure 43

Starting the Development Server 44

Conclusion 44

3.2 Generating Models, Views, and Controllers 44

Rails Generators 44

Running Migrations 45

Routes and Controllers 45

Conclusion 45

3.3 Configuring Routes 46

The `config/routes.rb` File 46

Basic Route Configuration 46

Route Parameters 46

Named Routes 46

Resourceful Routing 47

Route Constraints 47

Conclusion 47

3.4 Working with Databases in Rails 47

Database Configuration 47

Creating a Model 48

Running Migrations 48

Interacting with the Database 48

Seeding the Database 48

Database Queries 49

Conclusion 49

3.5 Adding Basic Styling with CSS 49

CSS in Rails 49

Adding Custom Styles 49

Asset Pipeline Directives 50

CSS Frameworks 50

Conclusion 50

Chapter 4: Working with Models and Databases 51

4.1 Understanding Active Record 51

The Active Record Pattern 51

CRUD Operations with Active Record 51

Active Record Associations 52

Migrations and Database Schema 52

Conclusion 52

4.2 Creating and Migrating Databases 52

Database Configuration 53

Creating a New Database 53

Database Migrations 53

Defining Database Changes 53

Running Migrations 54

Rollback and Redo 54

Conclusion 54

4.3 Defining Models and Associations 54

Creating a Model 55

Defining Model Associations 55

Customizing Associations 56

Database Migrations for Associations 56

Conclusion 56

4.4 Querying the Database 56

Basic Querying 56

Conditions and Filtering 57

Chaining Queries 57

Selecting Specific Columns 57

Aggregations 57

Using SQL Fragments 58

Conclusion 58

4.5 Validations and Callbacks in Rails Models 58

Validations...58

Callbacks...59

Custom Validations and Callbacks 59

Conclusion 60

Chapter 5: Crafting Beautiful Views with ERB and HAML........................61

5.1 Introduction to Views in Rails...61

Understanding Views...61

ERB (Embedded Ruby) 61

HAML (HTML Abstraction Markup Language)...................................62

Choosing Between ERB and HAML...62

Conclusion 62

5.2 Using ERB for Template Rendering 62

ERB Syntax 62

Accessing Controller Data..63

Rendering Partial Views 63

Layouts and Yield 63

Conclusion 64

5.3 Simplifying Views with HAML..64

Installing HAML..64

HAML Syntax 65

Interpolating Ruby Code 65

Conditional Statements and Loops 65

Partial Views in HAML...66

Advantages of HAML...66

Conclusion 66

5.4 Layouts and Partials 66

Layouts...66

Partials 67

Nested Partials..67

Conclusion 68

5.5 Working with Forms and Form Helpers 68

Creating Forms 68

Form Fields 69

Strong Parameters 69

Handling Form Submissions..69

Form Validation..69

Complex Forms...70

Conclusion 70

Chapter 6: Mastering Controllers and Routes 71

6.1 The Role of Controllers in Rails 71

The MVC Architecture Recap...71

Creating Controllers 71

Actions and Routes 71

Controller Actions 72

Rendering Views...72

Conclusion 73

6.2 Handling HTTP Requests..73

Routing in Rails 73

Request Parameters 73

Strong Parameters 74

Conclusion 75

6.3 Custom Routes and Route Constraints..75

Custom Routes..75

Route Constraints...75

Advanced Route Constraints 76

Dynamic Segments...76

Conclusion 77

6.4 Working with Filters and Middleware..77

Filters in Rails 77

Middleware in Rails..78

Conclusion 79

6.5 Implementing Authentication with Devise..79

What is Devise?...79

Adding Devise to Your Rails Application...79

Creating a User Model 80

Running Migrations..80

Configuring Routes 80

Customizing Views..80

Using Devise Helpers 80

Conclusion 81

Chapter 7: Testing Your Rails Application 82

7.1 The Importance of Testing in Rails 82

Why Testing Matters...82

Types of Tests in Rails..82

Writing Tests in Rails...83

Conclusion 83

7.2 Writing Unit Tests with RSpec 84

Why RSpec?...84

Setting Up RSpec 84

Writing Your First Unit Test 84

Running RSpec Tests...85

Additional RSpec Matchers 85

Conclusion 85

7.3 Integration Testing with Capybara 85

What is Capybara?..85

Setting Up Capybara...86

Writing Your First Capybara Test 86

Running Capybara Tests..86

Capybara Matchers 87

Choosing a Driver 87

Conclusion 87

7.4 Continuous Integration with Travis CI 87

What is Travis CI?..87

Setting Up Travis CI for Your Rails Project...87

Benefits of Travis CI 88

Conclusion 88

7.5 Debugging and Troubleshooting Techniques......................................89

1. Debugging Tools...89

2. Logging...89

3. Error Pages and Exception Handling 90

4. Database Queries 90

5. Third-Party Tools 90

6. Testing and Test-Driven Development (TDD) 90

7. Collaborate and Seek Help 91

Conclusion 91

Chapter 8: Enhancing Your Application with JavaScript and AJAX 92

8.1 Introduction to JavaScript in Rails 92

Why JavaScript in Rails? 92

Including JavaScript in Rails 92

Unobtrusive JavaScript 92

AJAX in Rails..93

Conclusion 94

8.2 Making AJAX Requests..94

1. Using `remote: true`..94

2. Handling AJAX Requests in the Controller...94

3. Updating the Page with JavaScript...95

4. Using Data Attributes..95

5. AJAX and Error Handling...95

Conclusion 96

8.3 Implementing Real-Time Features with WebSockets..96

1. The Need for Real-Time Features..96

2. Action Cable in Rails...96

3. Setting Up Action Cable..96

4. JavaScript Integration 97

5. Broadcasting Messages 98

6. Handling Multiple Channels..98

Conclusion 98

8.4 Using JavaScript Libraries (e.g., jQuery) 98

1. Integrating jQuery...98

2. Basic DOM Manipulation 99

3. Event Handling 99

4. AJAX Requests with jQuery 99

5. Working with Forms...100

6. jQuery Plugins and Enhancements...100

Conclusion...100

8.5 Front-End Frameworks and Integration with Rails...101

1. Choosing a Front-End Framework 101

2. Setting Up a Rails API 101

3. Front-End Integration 101

4. Building Front-End Components 102

5. Making API Requests 102

6. Authentication and Authorization 102

Conclusion 102

Chapter 9: RESTful API Development with Rails 104

9.1 Understanding RESTful Principles 104

1. Resource-Based 104

2. CRUD Operations 104

3. Stateless 104

4. Uniform Interface 104

5. Representation 104

6. HATEOAS (Hypermedia as the Engine of Application State) 105

Building RESTful APIs in Rails 105

9.2 Building API Endpoints 105

Defining API Routes 105

Creating API Controllers 105

Responding with JSON 107

Testing API Endpoints 107

9.3 Securing Your API with Authentication 107

1. Token-Based Authentication 107

2. OAuth 2.0 107

3. API Keys 108

4. JWT (JSON Web Tokens) 108

9.4 Versioning Your API 109

Why API Versioning? 109

1. URI Versioning 109

2. Accept Header Versioning 109

3. Subdomain Versioning 110

4. Request Parameter Versioning 110

Handling Multiple Versions 110

9.5 Documenting Your API with Swagger 110

What is Swagger?...111

Getting Started with Swagger in Ruby on Rails.........................111

Swagger UI Features..112

Conclusion...112

Chapter 10: Deploying Your Rails Application 112

Section 10.1: Preparing for Deployment 112

Section 10.2: Choosing a Hosting Provider 114

1. Heroku 114

2. AWS (Amazon Web Services) 115

3. DigitalOcean 115

4. Google Cloud Platform (GCP)...116

5. Microsoft Azure...116

6. Other Options...116

Conclusion...116

Section 10.3: Setting Up Production Environment 117

1. Web Server Configuration..117

2. Application Server 117

3. Database Setup...118

4. Environment Variables...118

5. Monitoring and Logging..118

6. Deployment Scripts...118

7. Scaling 118

Conclusion...118

Section 10.4: Deploying with Capistrano 119

Installation...119

Configuration..119

Deploying Your Application 119

Custom Tasks...120

Rollbacks 120

Conclusion...120

Section 10.5: Scaling and Monitoring Your Rails App............120

Scaling Your Rails Application 120

Monitoring Your Rails Application..121

Autoscaling 122

Load Testing...122

Conclusion...122

Chapter 11: Performance Optimization...123

Section 11.1: Identifying Performance Bottlenecks 123

Monitoring and Profiling 123

Common Bottlenecks 123

Section 11.2: Caching Strategies in Rails..123

Page Caching 124

Action Caching...124

Fragment Caching...124

Key-Based Caching..124

Caching Stores...124

Section 11.3: Database Optimization Techniques 124

Indexing 124

Database Migrations...124

Query Optimization..124

Connection Pooling 125

Section 11.4: Load Balancing and Scaling 125

Load Balancers...125

Horizontal Scaling...125

Vertical Scaling..125

Section 11.5: Profiling and Benchmarking Your Application 125

Ruby Profiling...125

Benchmarking...125

Continuous Performance Testing 125

Chapter 11: Performance Optimization...126

Section 11.1: Identifying Performance Bottlenecks 126

Monitoring and Profiling 126

Common Bottlenecks 126

Example: Identifying N+1 Query Problems...126

Section 11.2: Caching Strategies in Rails..127

1. Page Caching 127

2. Action Caching..127

3. Fragment Caching..128

4. Model Caching 128

5. HTTP Caching 128

Section 11.3: Database Optimization Techniques 129

1. Indexing..129

2. Query Optimization...129

3. Database Connection Pooling 129

4. Avoid N+1 Query Problem 129

5. Database Sharding...130

6. Use Caching..130

7. Regular Maintenance 130

Section 11.4: Load Balancing and Scaling 130

Load Balancing..130

Horizontal Scaling...131

Vertical Scaling..131

Auto-Scaling 132

Monitoring and Alerts..132

Section 11.5: Profiling and Benchmarking Your Application 132

Profiling Your Rails Application 132

Benchmarking Your Rails Application..133

Interpreting Results..133

Chapter 12: Security Best Practices..135

Section 12.1: Common Web Application Security Threats..................135

1. Cross-Site Scripting (XSS)..135

2. Cross-Site Request Forgery (CSRF)..135

3. SQL Injection 135

4. Insecure Authentication..135

5. Insecure File Uploads 136

6. Security Misconfigurations 136

7. Lack of Session Management 136

8. Broken Authentication...136

9. Data Exposure 136

10. Unvalidated Redirects and Forwards..136

Section 12.2: Cross-Site Scripting (XSS) Protection..........................137

1. Output Encoding...137

2. Whitelisting and Sanitization..137

3. Content Security Policy (CSP)..137

4. Escaping JavaScript...138

5. Reflected and Stored XSS...138

Section 12.3: Cross-Site Request Forgery (CSRF) Prevention...................138

1. Rails CSRF Protection...138

2. Handling Ajax Requests..139

3. Same-Site Cookies..139

Section 12.4: SQL Injection and Parameterization....................................140

1. Active Record and Parameterization..140

2. Strong Parameters..140

3. Sanitizing Input..141

4. Regular Security Audits..141

Section 12.5: Securing File Uploads and Authentication..........................141

1. Secure File Uploads..142

2. Authentication and Authorization..143

Chapter 13: Internationalization and Localization......................................145

Section 13.1: Making Your App Multilingual...145

1. Set Up Internationalization (i18n)..145

2. Translate Your Application..145

3. Use Translation Helpers...146

4. Dynamic Locale Switching..146

Section 13.2: Working with Translation Files...146

Organizing Translation Files...146

Using Interpolations..147

Pluralization..147

Section 13.3: Dynamic Content Localization...148

Setting the Locale..148

Localizing Dates and Times...148

Localizing Numbers...148

Translating Dynamic Content..149

Section 13.4: Language and Region Detection...149

Browser-Based Language Detection..149

Using Geolocation for Region Detection...149

Storing User Preferences...150

Providing Language and Region Selection......................................150

Section 13.5: Handling Time Zones in Rails....................................150

Rails' Built-in Time Zone Support...151

Displaying Time in Views...151

Daylight Saving Time...152

Time Zone Database Updates..152

Chapter 14: Advanced Topics in Rails..152

Section 14.1: Background Jobs with Active Job.............................152

Section 14.2: Building a Real-Time Chat Application....................154

WebSocket and Rails...154

Getting Started...154

Section 14.3: Implementing Single Sign-On (SSO).......................155

The Benefits of SSO..155

Implementing SSO in Rails...156

Section 14.4: GraphQL with Ruby on Rails...................................157

Understanding GraphQL..157

Implementing GraphQL in Rails..157

Section 14.5: Exploring Microservices Architecture....................158

The Microservices Philosophy..159

Implementing Microservices in Ruby on Rails.............................159

Chapter 15: Version Control and Collaboration............................161

Section 15.1: Git Essentials for Rails Developers..........................161

What is Git?...161

Key Git Concepts..161

Using Git in Rails Development..162

Git Hosting Services..163

Section 15.2: Collaborating with Git and GitHub........................163

Forking a Repository...163

Cloning a Forked Repository..163

Adding a Remote...164

Making Changes and Committing...164

Pushing Changes to Your Fork...164

Creating a Pull Request...164

Reviewing and Merging Pull Requests 165

Keeping Your Fork in Sync...165

Section 15.3: Managing Feature Branches..165

Creating a Feature Branch 166

Working on the Feature 166

Collaborative Development..166

Merging the Feature 167

Summary...167

Section 15.4: Code Reviews and Best Practices...167

Why Code Reviews Matter...167

Best Practices for Code Reviews 168

Code Review Workflow..169

Conclusion...169

Section 15.5: Resolving Merge Conflicts..169

Understanding Merge Conflicts 169

Why Merge Conflicts Occur 170

Resolving Merge Conflicts...170

Conflict Resolution Tools...171

Conflict Prevention 171

Chapter 16: Continuous Learning and Resources 172

Section 16.1: Staying Up-to-Date with Rails 172

1. Official Rails Documentation...172

2. Rails Release Notes...172

3. Rails Mailing List and Forums 172

4. Blogs and Newsletters 172

5. Podcasts and Webinars 172

6. Social Media and GitHub 173

7. Online Courses and Books..173

8. Conferences and Meetups 173

9. Online Communities 173

10. Open Source Contributions...173

11. Experiment and Build..173

Section 16.2: Joining the Rails Community...173

1. Attend Local Meetups...174

2. Engage on Online Platforms 174

3. Contribute to Open Source 174

4. Attend Rails Conferences 174

5. Join the Rails Core Team 174

6. Engage on Social Media 174

7. Organize Your Own Events 174

8. Collaborate on Projects 175

9. Write Blog Posts and Documentation 175

10. Be Supportive and Inclusive 175

Section 16.3: Recommended Blogs and Podcasts 175

Blogs 175

Podcasts 176

Section 16.4: Books and Online Courses 176

Books 177

Online Courses 177

Section 16.5: Contributing to Open Source Rails Projects 178

Why Contribute to Open Source? 178

How to Contribute 178

Finding Open Source Rails Projects 179

Chapter 17: Building and Launching Your Portfolio 180

Section 17.1: Creating a Portfolio Website 180

Section 17.2: Showcasing Your Projects 182

Section 17.3: Writing a Developer Blog 184

Section 17.4: Networking and Job Hunting Tips 185

Section 17.5: Preparing for Job Interviews 187

Chapter 18: Case Studies and Real-World Projects 190

Section 18.1: Case Study 1: Building an E-commerce Platform 190

Understanding the Requirements 190

Database Design 190

Implementing User Authentication 190

Building the Product Catalog 190

Shopping Cart and Checkout 191

Order Processing 191

Admin Panel 191

Security Measures 191

Scalability 191

Testing and Quality Assurance 191

Launch and Maintenance...191

Section 18.2: Case Study 2: Creating a Social Networking App 192

Understanding the Requirements 192

Database Design 192

Implementing User Authentication 192

User Profiles and Avatars..192

Post Creation and Feeds 192

Social Interactions 193

Messaging System...193

Content Moderation...193

Responsive Design...193

Testing and Quality Assurance 193

Launch and Maintenance...193

Section 18.3: Case Study 3: Developing a SaaS Application 193

Concept and Planning 194

Multi-Tenancy Architecture 194

User Authentication and Roles...194

Subscription Billing...194

User Onboarding 194

Feature Development..194

Data Analytics and Insights 194

Scalability and Performance 194

Security and Compliance 195

Testing and Quality Assurance 195

Documentation and Support...195

Continuous Deployment and Monitoring...195

User Feedback and Iteration...195

Section 18.4: Case Study 4: Building a Content Management System 195

Planning and Requirements..195

Data Modeling 196

Authentication and Authorization...196

Content Creation and Editing 196

Categories and Tags..196

Content Publishing and Scheduling 196

SEO and URL Handling 197

Media Management..197

User-Friendly Interface 197

Security and Access Control...197

Scalability and Performance 197

Testing and Quality Assurance 197

Documentation and User Support..197

Section 18.5: Lessons Learned from Real-World Projects...198

1. Planning and Requirements Gathering 198

2. Choosing the Right Gems 198

3. Database Optimization 198

4. Testing and Test Coverage..198

5. Continuous Integration 198

6. Code Review...198

7. Security Best Practices..198

8. Scalability 198

9. Documentation and Knowledge Sharing 198

10. User Experience (UX) and Feedback...199

11. Version Control and Collaboration 199

12. Error Monitoring and Logging..199

13. Performance Profiling 199

14. Backup and Disaster Recovery 199

15. Feedback Loops and Retrospectives..199

16. Community and Resources 199

17. Adaptability and Flexibility...199

18. Project Management and Communication 199

19. Taking Breaks and Avoiding Burnout 199

20. Celebrating Successes...199

Chapter 19: Future Trends in Rails Development...201

Section 19.1: The Evolution of Ruby on Rails...201

1. API-First Development 201

2. JavaScript Integration 201

3. Performance Optimization...201

4. Microservices and Modularization 201

5. Containerization and Docker 201

6. Serverless Computing 201

7. WebAssembly (Wasm) 202

8. Progressive Web Apps (PWAs)..202

9. AI and Machine Learning..202

10. Community Contributions..202

Section 19.2: WebAssembly and Rails...202

What is WebAssembly?...202

Using WebAssembly in Rails..202

Potential Use Cases 203

Section 19.3: Progressive Web Apps (PWAs)...204

What are Progressive Web Apps?..204

Building PWAs with Ruby on Rails 204

Benefits of PWAs...205

Considerations 206

Section 19.4: Serverless Architecture with Rails 206

Understanding Serverless Architecture...206

Integrating Serverless with Ruby on Rails..206

Benefits of Serverless with Rails...207

Section 19.5: Exploring AI and Machine Learning in Rails Apps 208

AI and ML in Web Development...208

Integrating AI/ML in Rails 208

Benefits of AI/ML in Rails 209

Chapter 20: Conclusion and Next Steps 211

Section 20.1: Reflecting on Your Journey...211

Celebrating Your Achievements...211

Setting Future Goals 211

Embracing Lifelong Learning 211

Final Thoughts 212

Section 20.2: Setting Future Goals as a Rails Developer..212

1. Advanced Specialization 212

2. Contributions to Open Source...212

3. Continuous Learning...212

4. Certifications..213

5. Entrepreneurship..213

6. Mentorship and Teaching...213

7. Networking..213

8. Diversity in Your Portfolio...213

9. Remote Work and Freelancing..213

10. Contribution to the Ruby on Rails Community.....................................213

Section 20.3: Resources for Advanced Learning..214

1. Advanced Rails Books...214

2. Rails Blogs and Newsletters...214

3. Online Courses and Tutorials...214

4. Advanced Ruby and Rails Podcasts..214

5. Advanced Ruby and Rails Conferences..214

6. Advanced Ruby Gems..214

7. Advanced Testing Tools..214

8. Advanced Deployment and DevOps...215

9. Contributing to Open Source..215

10. Advanced Meetups and Communities..215

Section 20.4: Final Thoughts and Farewell..215

Reflecting on Your Progress...215

The Ongoing Learning Process...215

Setting Future Goals...215

Contributing to the Community..216

Staying Inspired..216

Farewell and Thank You..216

Section 20.5: Acknowledgments and Credits...216

Contributors..216

Open Source Projects..216

Publishing Team..217

Special Thanks..217

Your Support...217

Chapter 1: Introduction to Ruby on Rails

1.1 What is Ruby on Rails?

Ruby on Rails, often simply referred to as Rails, is a powerful and elegant web application framework written in the Ruby programming language. It was created by David Heinemeier Hansson (DHH) and was first released in 2005. Rails follows the Model-View-Controller (MVC) architectural pattern, which promotes clean, organized, and maintainable code.

History of Ruby on Rails

To understand Ruby on Rails better, let's take a brief look at its history. Rails was extracted from Basecamp, a project management tool developed by 37signals (now known as Basecamp). DHH, while working on Basecamp, realized the need for a more efficient and developer-friendly framework to build web applications quickly. He open-sourced Rails, and it gained popularity rapidly due to its developer-friendly philosophy and convention over configuration (CoC) approach.

Key Features of Ruby on Rails

Ruby on Rails is known for its simplicity and developer-friendly features. Some key features include:

1. **Convention Over Configuration (CoC):** Rails follows sensible conventions, reducing the need for developers to make unnecessary decisions about project structure and configuration.

2. **Don't Repeat Yourself (DRY) Principle:** Rails encourages writing reusable code and avoiding duplication through the DRY principle.

3. **Rapid Development:** Rails provides built-in tools for scaffolding, code generation, and automation, allowing developers to create fully functional applications quickly.

4. **Active Record:** Rails includes an Object-Relational Mapping (ORM) library called Active Record, which simplifies database interactions and relationships between objects.

5. **Rich Ecosystem:** Rails has a vast community and a rich ecosystem of gems (Ruby libraries) that extend its functionality, making it easy to add features to your application.

6. **Security:** Rails includes built-in security features to protect against common web vulnerabilities, such as SQL injection and Cross-Site Scripting (XSS).

Setting Up Your Development Environment

Before you can start building Rails applications, you need to set up your development environment. Here are the basic steps:

1. **Install Ruby:** Rails is built on the Ruby programming language, so you need to have Ruby installed. You can use tools like RVM (Ruby Version Manager) or rbenv to manage your Ruby versions.

2. **Install Rails:** Once you have Ruby installed, you can install Rails using the gem package manager. Run `gem install rails` in your terminal.

3. **Database Setup:** Rails typically uses relational databases like PostgreSQL, MySQL, or SQLite. You'll need to install and configure one of these databases for your project.

4. **Text Editor or IDE:** Choose a text editor or integrated development environment (IDE) for writing your Rails code. Popular choices include Visual Studio Code, Sublime Text, and RubyMine.

5. **Version Control:** Set up version control for your project using Git. Create a Git repository to track changes in your code.

6. **Web Server:** Rails applications need a web server to serve web pages. The built-in server, WEBrick, is suitable for development, but you may use more robust options like Puma or Unicorn in production.

Hello World in Rails

Let's create a simple "Hello, World!" application in Rails to get a taste of how it works. Open your terminal and run the following commands:

```
# Create a new Rails application
rails new hello_rails

# Navigate to the project directory
cd hello_rails

# Generate a controller and a view
rails generate controller welcome index

# Edit the view file app/views/welcome/index.html.erb
```

In the app/views/welcome/index.html.erb file, add the following code:

```
<!DOCTYPE html>
<html>
  <head>
    <title>Hello Rails</title>
  </head>
```

```
<body>
    <h1>Hello, Rails!</h1>
  </body>
</html>
```

Now, start the Rails server:

```
rails server
```

Visit http://localhost:3000 in your web browser, and you should see your "Hello, Rails!" message. This is a basic Rails application in action.

The MVC Architecture in Rails

Ruby on Rails follows the Model-View-Controller (MVC) architectural pattern. This separation of concerns helps organize your code and maintainability.

- **Model:** The model represents the data and business logic of the application. It interacts with the database and handles data validation and manipulation.

- **View:** The view is responsible for presenting data to users. It defines the user interface and templates for rendering data.

- **Controller:** The controller handles incoming requests, processes them, interacts with the model, and renders the appropriate view. It acts as an intermediary between the model and the view.

In Rails, these components work together to create dynamic and interactive web applications. The MVC pattern encourages a clean and modular codebase, making it easier to maintain and extend your projects.

This chapter has provided an overview of Ruby on Rails, its history, key features, and the initial steps to set up your development environment and create a simple application. In the following chapters, we will delve deeper into each aspect of Rails development, building a solid foundation for your journey as a Rails developer.

1.2 A Brief History of Ruby on Rails

Ruby on Rails, often referred to as Rails, has a rich and influential history in the world of web development. Understanding its evolution and the key milestones in its development can provide valuable context for developers and enthusiasts.

Birth of Ruby on Rails

The story of Ruby on Rails begins with its creator, David Heinemeier Hansson (DHH). In 2003, while working on the development of the project management tool Basecamp at 37signals (now Basecamp), DHH started working on a web application framework to simplify the development process. He extracted this framework from the codebase of Basecamp and open-sourced it in July 2004.

The framework was initially just called "Rails" and was designed to work with the Ruby programming language. It quickly gained popularity among developers for its elegant and productive approach to building web applications. The combination of Ruby's expressiveness and Rails' conventions made it an attractive choice for web development.

Release of Ruby on Rails 1.0

On December 13, 2005, Ruby on Rails reached a significant milestone with the release of version 1.0. This marked the official stability and maturity of the framework. Rails 1.0 introduced a range of features, including a comprehensive testing framework (Test::Unit), AJAX support with the Prototype library, and support for multiple database management systems.

The release of Rails 1.0 solidified its reputation as a framework that emphasized developer productivity and creativity while maintaining best practices.

The Rise of the Rails Community

One of the strengths of Ruby on Rails has been its vibrant and inclusive community. Developers from around the world contributed to the framework, creating a wealth of open-source libraries (gems) that extended Rails' capabilities. This ecosystem of gems allowed developers to easily add features to their applications and leverage the work of others.

In addition to the open-source community, a strong commercial ecosystem emerged around Rails. Companies began to offer hosting, support, and consulting services for Rails applications, further driving its adoption.

The Rails Doctrine and Philosophy

Ruby on Rails is not just a framework; it has a philosophy and a set of guiding principles known as the "Rails Doctrine." The Rails Doctrine includes concepts such as Convention over Configuration (CoC), Don't Repeat Yourself (DRY), and the pursuit of developer happiness. These principles emphasize the importance of simplicity, automation, and reducing unnecessary decisions in the development process.

Major Versions and Improvements

Over the years, Ruby on Rails has seen multiple major releases, each introducing new features and improvements. Some notable versions include:

- **Rails 2.0 (December 2007):** Introduced RESTful routing, which aligned Rails applications with the principles of Representational State Transfer (REST).

- **Rails 3.0 (August 2010):** Included a major revamp of the framework, with improved modularity and better support for web services.

- **Rails 4.0 (June 2013):** Added support for Russian Doll Caching and introduced the Turbolinks feature for faster page rendering.

- **Rails 5.0 (June 2016):** Introduced the Action Cable framework for handling WebSockets and real-time features.

- **Rails 6.0 (August 2019):** Brought enhancements like Action Mailbox for processing incoming emails and Action Text for rich text content.

The Continuing Evolution

As of my knowledge cutoff date in September 2021, Ruby on Rails continues to evolve. The community remains active, and new versions are regularly released to address security issues, improve performance, and provide new features. Rails remains a popular choice for web developers, known for its developer-friendly nature and the productivity it offers.

This brief history provides a glimpse into the origins and growth of Ruby on Rails, from its humble beginnings as an internal tool to becoming a widely adopted and influential web development framework. Understanding this history can help developers appreciate the principles and values that have shaped Rails into what it is today.

1.3 Setting Up Your Development Environment

Before you can start building Ruby on Rails applications, it's essential to set up your development environment properly. A well-configured environment ensures that you have all the necessary tools and dependencies to work with Rails efficiently. This section will guide you through the steps required to set up your development environment.

1.3.1 Installing Ruby

Ruby is the programming language on which Ruby on Rails is built. To get started, you need to have Ruby installed on your system. There are various methods for installing Ruby, but one of the most popular ways is to use a version manager such as RVM (Ruby Version Manager) or rbenv. These tools allow you to manage multiple Ruby versions on your machine.

Installing Ruby with RVM

To install Ruby using RVM, follow these steps:

1. **Install RVM:** Open your terminal and run the following command to install RVM:

   ```
   \curl -sSL https://get.rvm.io | bash -s stable
   ```

2. **Close and Reopen Terminal:** After RVM is installed, close and reopen your terminal window to ensure that the RVM commands are available.

3. **Install Ruby:** Install the desired Ruby version. For example, to install Ruby 3.0.2, run:

```
rvm install 3.0.2
```

4. **Set Default Ruby Version:** Make the installed Ruby version your default:

```
rvm use 3.0.2 --default
```

Installing Ruby with rbenv

To install Ruby using rbenv, follow these steps:

1. **Install rbenv:** Open your terminal and run the following commands to install rbenv and the rbenv-build plugin:

```
brew install rbenv
brew install rbenv-build
```

2. **Initialize rbenv:** Add the following to your shell profile (e.g., ~/.zshrc or ~/.bashrc):

```
if which rbenv > /dev/null; then eval "$(rbenv init -)"; fi
```

3. **Close and Reopen Terminal:** After adding the above line to your shell profile, close and reopen your terminal to ensure that rbenv is properly initialized.

4. **Install Ruby:** Install the desired Ruby version. For example, to install Ruby 3.0.2, run:

```
rbenv install 3.0.2
```

5. **Set Global Ruby Version:** Set the global Ruby version to the one you installed:

```
rbenv global 3.0.2
```

1.3.2 Installing Rails

With Ruby installed, you can now proceed to install Ruby on Rails. Rails can be installed using the RubyGems package manager, which comes with Ruby.

1. **Install Rails:** Open your terminal and run the following command to install the latest version of Ruby on Rails:

```
gem install rails
```

2. **Verify Installation:** After installation, you can verify that Rails was installed correctly by running:

```
rails --version
```

This command should display the installed Rails version.

1.3.3 Database Setup

Ruby on Rails typically works with relational databases such as PostgreSQL, MySQL, or SQLite. You'll need to have a database system installed on your development machine and configure your Rails application to use it.

Installing PostgreSQL (Example)

For PostgreSQL, you can use a package manager like Homebrew (on macOS and Linux) to install it. Here are the steps for macOS:

1. **Install Homebrew:** If you don't have Homebrew installed, follow the installation instructions on the Homebrew website.

2. **Install PostgreSQL:** Run the following command to install PostgreSQL:

   ```
   brew install postgresql
   ```

3. **Start PostgreSQL:** Start the PostgreSQL service:

   ```
   brew services start postgresql
   ```

Configuring Database in Rails

In your Rails application, database configuration is defined in the `config/database.yml` file. You'll need to update this file to specify the database connection details, such as the username and password.

1.3.4 Text Editor or IDE

Choose a text editor or integrated development environment (IDE) for writing your Rails code. Some popular choices among Rails developers include Visual Studio Code, Sublime Text, Atom, and RubyMine. These tools offer various features and extensions to enhance your development experience.

1.3.5 Version Control

Version control is crucial for tracking changes in your code and collaborating with others. Git is the most widely used version control system, and platforms like GitHub, GitLab, and Bitbucket provide hosting and collaboration features.

If you're new to Git, it's a good idea to learn the basics of Git commands, such as `git init`, `git clone`, `git add`, `git commit`, and `git push`.

1.3.6 Web Server

Rails applications need a web server to serve web pages to users. While Rails includes a built-in server called WEBrick, it's primarily used for development purposes. In production, you'll typically use more robust web servers like Puma, Unicorn, or Phusion Passenger.

Conclusion

Setting up your development environment is a crucial initial step on your Ruby on Rails journey. With Ruby, Rails, a database, a text editor or IDE, version control, and a web server in place, you're well-prepared to start building web applications with Ruby on Rails. In the next chapters, we'll dive deeper into Rails development, covering various aspects of building and deploying applications.

1.4 Hello World in Rails

In this section, you'll embark on a hands-on journey by creating a simple "Hello, World!" application in Ruby on Rails. This basic project will introduce you to the fundamental structure of a Rails application and help you understand how various components work together.

Creating a New Rails Project

To begin, open your terminal and navigate to the directory where you want to create your Rails application. Run the following command to generate a new Rails project:

```
rails new hello_world
```

This command creates a new directory named `hello_world` containing the initial files and folders of your Rails application. It also installs the necessary dependencies.

Exploring the Project Structure

Let's take a moment to explore the basic structure of a newly generated Rails application:

- **app:** This directory is where most of your application's code resides. It contains subdirectories for models, views, and controllers.

- **config:** Configuration files for your application, including `routes.rb` (for defining URL routes), `database.yml` (for database configuration), and `application.rb` (for general application settings).

- **db:** This directory is used for database-related files, including migrations, schema, and seeds.

- **public:** Static files like images, stylesheets, and JavaScript files are stored here.

- **Gemfile:** Specifies the gems (libraries) that your application depends on. You can add or remove gems to customize your project.

- **Rakefile:** Defines tasks that can be run with the `rake` command. Rails uses Rake for various tasks, such as database migrations.

- **README.md:** A README file for your application, typically containing information about how to set up and use the project.

Generating a Controller and View

Next, let's create a controller and view to display our "Hello, World!" message. In Rails, controllers handle incoming requests and render views. Run the following command to generate a controller named `welcome` with an action called `index`:

```
rails generate controller welcome index
```

This command generates the necessary files for the `welcome` controller and an `index` view.

Editing the View

Now, navigate to the `app/views/welcome` directory and open the `index.html.erb` file. This file contains the HTML content that will be rendered when you access the `welcome#index` action. Replace the contents of `index.html.erb` with the following code:

```html
<!DOCTYPE html>
<html>
  <head>
    <title>Hello, World!</title>
  </head>
  <body>
    <h1>Hello, World!</h1>
  </body>
</html>
```

This simple HTML code displays an "Hello, World!" message when you visit the corresponding route.

Starting the Rails Server

To see your "Hello, World!" application in action, start the Rails server by running the following command in your terminal:

```
rails server
```

The server will start, and you can access your application by opening a web browser and visiting http://localhost:3000. You should see the "Hello, World!" message displayed in your browser.

Understanding the Route

In this "Hello, World!" example, the route that maps to the `welcome#index` action is defined in the `config/routes.rb` file. It looks like this:

```ruby
# config/routes.rb
Rails.application.routes.draw do
  get 'welcome/index'
```

```
  root 'welcome#index'
end
```

The `get 'welcome/index'` line specifies that when you visit the URL `/welcome/index`, the `welcome#index` action should be called. The `root 'welcome#index'` line designates the `welcome#index` action as the root route, which means it will be the default page when you visit the root URL (http://localhost:3000).

Conclusion

Congratulations! You've created your first Ruby on Rails application and displayed a "Hello, World!" message. This simple example demonstrates the essential components of a Rails application, including controllers, views, routes, and the development server. As you continue to explore Rails, you'll dive deeper into building more complex and feature-rich web applications.

1.5 The MVC Architecture in Rails

Ruby on Rails (Rails) follows the Model-View-Controller (MVC) architectural pattern, which is crucial to understanding how Rails applications are structured and how they handle requests and responses.

Understanding MVC

MVC is an architectural pattern that separates an application into three interconnected components:

- **Model:** The Model represents the application's data and business logic. In Rails, Models are responsible for interacting with the database, performing data validation, and handling data manipulation. Each Model typically corresponds to a database table and contains the rules for how data is retrieved, stored, and manipulated.

- **View:** The View is responsible for presenting the data to the user. It defines the user interface and templates for rendering data. In Rails, Views use embedded Ruby (ERB) or other templating engines to generate dynamic HTML that is sent to the user's browser.

- **Controller:** The Controller handles incoming HTTP requests, processes them, interacts with the Model to fetch or manipulate data, and selects the appropriate View to render the response. Controllers are responsible for managing the flow of the application, handling user input, and making decisions based on that input.

How MVC Works in Rails

In a Rails application, MVC is implemented as follows:

- **Model:** Each Model in Rails is typically a Ruby class that inherits from ActiveRecord::Base, which is part of the Active Record library. Active Record provides a convenient and object-oriented way to interact with databases. Models define database tables and establish associations between them. They also handle tasks like data validation and callbacks.

  Example of a simple Rails Model:

  ```ruby
  # app/models/user.rb
  class User < ApplicationRecord
    validates :username, presence: true, uniqueness: true
    has_many :posts
  end
  ```

- **View:** Views in Rails are responsible for presenting the data to users. They are typically HTML templates with embedded Ruby code that allows dynamic rendering of data. Views can be simple, such as rendering plain HTML, or they can involve complex logic and partials for reusable components.

  Example of a simple Rails View:

  ```erb
  <!-- app/views/posts/index.html.erb -->
  <h1>List of Posts</h1>
  <ul>
    <% @posts.each do |post| %>
      <li><%= post.title %></li>
    <% end %>
  </ul>
  ```

- **Controller:** Controllers in Rails are Ruby classes that inherit from ApplicationController. They define actions that correspond to different routes and HTTP methods. Controllers handle incoming requests, process parameters, interact with Models to fetch or manipulate data, and render Views. They serve as the bridge between the Model and View components.

  Example of a simple Rails Controller:

  ```ruby
  # app/controllers/posts_controller.rb
  class PostsController < ApplicationController
    def index
      @posts = Post.all
    end
  end
  ```

Routing in Rails

Routing in Rails is responsible for mapping incoming HTTP requests to the appropriate Controller actions. Routes are defined in the `config/routes.rb` file, and they determine which Controller and action should handle a specific URL.

Example of defining a route in Rails:

```ruby
# config/routes.rb
Rails.application.routes.draw do
  get '/posts', to: 'posts#index'
  # ...
end
```

In this example, a GET request to the /posts URL is mapped to the index action of the PostsController. When a user visits /posts in their browser, the index action is executed, and the associated View is rendered.

Benefits of MVC in Rails

The MVC architecture in Rails provides several advantages:

1. **Separation of Concerns:** MVC enforces a clear separation of concerns, making it easier to maintain and understand the codebase. Models, Views, and Controllers have distinct responsibilities.

2. **Reusability:** Views and Controllers can be reused with different Models, promoting code reusability. For example, you can have multiple Views that render data from the same Controller but present it differently.

3. **Testability:** Each component can be tested independently. Models can be tested for data validation and database interactions, Controllers can be tested for request handling, and Views can be tested for proper rendering.

4. **Scalability:** As an application grows, you can add more Controllers, Views, and Models to accommodate new features. The separation of concerns makes it easier to scale and maintain the application.

Understanding the MVC architecture is fundamental to building robust and maintainable Rails applications. It promotes clean code, efficient development, and effective collaboration among developers working on different parts of the application. As you delve deeper into Rails development, you'll find that MVC forms the foundation upon which you build dynamic and interactive web applications.

Chapter 2: Getting Started with Ruby

2.1 Understanding Ruby Syntax

Ruby is known for its elegant and concise syntax, which makes it a developer-friendly language. In this section, we'll explore the fundamental aspects of Ruby syntax, including variables, data types, control flow, and more.

Variables and Data Types

Variable Declaration

In Ruby, you can declare variables without explicitly specifying their data types. Variable names are case-sensitive and typically start with a lowercase letter or an underscore.

```
name = "Alice"
age = 30
```

Dynamic Typing

Ruby is dynamically typed, meaning that variable types are determined at runtime. You can change the type of a variable by assigning a new value to it.

```
x = 10
x = "hello"
```

Data Types

Ruby has several built-in data types, including:

- **Integer:** Represents whole numbers (e.g., 5, -42).
- **Float:** Represents decimal numbers (e.g., 3.14, -0.5).
- **String:** Represents text (e.g., "Hello, Ruby!").
- **Boolean:** Represents true or false values.
- **Array:** Ordered collections of values.
- **Hash:** Key-value pairs.

```
age = 25
pi = 3.14159
message = "Hello, Ruby!"
is_active = true
fruits = ["apple", "banana", "cherry"]
person = { "name" => "Alice", "age" => 30 }
```

Control Flow and Loops

Conditional Statements

Ruby uses if, else, and elsif for conditional statements.

```ruby
if age >= 18
  puts "You are an adult."
else
  puts "You are not an adult."
end
```

Loops

Ruby provides several loop constructs, including `while`, `until`, `for`, and iterators like `each`.

```ruby
# Using a while loop
counter = 0
while counter < 5
  puts "Counter is #{counter}"
  counter += 1
end
```

```ruby
# Using an each iterator
fruits = ["apple", "banana", "cherry"]
fruits.each do |fruit|
  puts "I like #{fruit}"
end
```

Strings and String Interpolation

String Concatenation

You can concatenate strings using the + operator or the << operator.

```ruby
first_name = "John"
last_name = "Doe"
full_name = first_name + " " + last_name
```

String Interpolation

Ruby allows you to embed expressions within double-quoted strings using #{}.

```ruby
name = "Alice"
greeting = "Hello, #{name}!"
```

Symbols

Symbols in Ruby are lightweight identifiers that are often used as keys in hashes. They are created by prefixing a word with a colon.

```ruby
status = :success
```

Symbols are more memory-efficient than strings and are typically used for keys that don't need to be modified.

Comments

Ruby supports both single-line and multi-line comments.

```
# This is a single-line comment

=begin
This is a
multi-line comment
=end
```

Conclusion

Understanding Ruby syntax is a crucial first step in your journey as a Ruby developer. In this section, we've covered variable declaration, data types, control flow, loops, strings, symbols, and comments. With a solid grasp of these fundamentals, you're well-equipped to start writing Ruby code and exploring more advanced topics as you continue your Ruby programming journey.

2.2 Variables and Data Types

Variables and data types are fundamental concepts in Ruby that allow you to store and manipulate information in your programs. In this section, we'll delve deeper into how to work with variables and explore the various data types available in Ruby.

Variable Assignment

In Ruby, you assign values to variables using the assignment operator (=). Variable names are case-sensitive, and they can contain letters, numbers, and underscores. A variable name cannot begin with a number.

```
name = "Alice"
age = 30
```

Ruby's dynamic typing allows you to change the value and data type of a variable during runtime:

```
x = 10
x = "hello"
```

Data Types in Ruby

Ruby supports a variety of data types, and it automatically determines the data type based on the assigned value. Some common data types in Ruby include:

- **Integer:** Represents whole numbers (e.g., 5, -42).
- **Float:** Represents decimal numbers (e.g., 3.14, -0.5).
- **String:** Represents text (e.g., "Hello, Ruby!").

- **Boolean:** Represents true or false values.
- **Array:** An ordered collection of values.
- **Hash:** A collection of key-value pairs.

```
age = 25
pi = 3.14159
message = "Hello, Ruby!"
is_active = true
fruits = ["apple", "banana", "cherry"]
person = { "name" => "Alice", "age" => 30 }
```

Type Conversion

You can convert between different data types in Ruby using various methods. For example, you can convert a string to an integer using the to_i method:

```
age_as_string = "25"
age_as_integer = age_as_string.to_i
```

Strings and String Manipulation

Strings in Ruby are sequences of characters, and they are enclosed in either single (") or double ("") quotes. Ruby provides various methods for manipulating strings, such as concatenation, interpolation, and substring extraction.

```
first_name = "John"
last_name = "Doe"
full_name = first_name + " " + last_name

greeting = "Hello, #{first_name}!"
```

Symbols

Symbols are lightweight identifiers in Ruby, often used as keys in hash data structures. Symbols are created by prefixing a word with a colon.

```
status = :success
```

Symbols are immutable and memory-efficient compared to strings, making them a preferred choice for keys in situations where the key doesn't need to be modified.

Constants

Constants in Ruby are defined with an initial uppercase letter and are used to store values that should not be changed throughout the program's execution.

```
PI = 3.14159
```

While Ruby allows you to modify constants, it will issue a warning if you do so. It's considered good practice not to change constants once they are defined.

Conclusion

Understanding variables and data types is foundational to writing Ruby code. In this section, we explored variable assignment, common data types, type conversion, string manipulation, symbols, and constants. These concepts provide you with the building blocks to create more complex programs and manipulate data effectively in your Ruby applications. As you progress, you'll use these fundamentals to tackle more advanced coding challenges and develop robust software solutions.

2.3 Control Flow and Loops

Control flow and loops are essential for directing the flow of your Ruby programs and performing repetitive tasks. In this section, we'll explore conditional statements, loops, and iterators, which are crucial for creating dynamic and responsive applications.

Conditional Statements

Conditional statements allow you to execute different blocks of code based on specific conditions. Ruby provides `if`, `else`, and `elsif` statements for this purpose.

The `if` Statement

The `if` statement evaluates a condition and executes a block of code if the condition is true.

```ruby
age = 20
if age >= 18
  puts "You are an adult."
end
```

The `else` Statement

The `else` statement is used with `if` to specify a block of code to execute when the condition is false.

```ruby
age = 15
if age >= 18
  puts "You are an adult."
else
  puts "You are not an adult."
end
```

The `elsif` Statement

The `elsif` statement is used to specify additional conditions to test if the initial `if` condition is false.

```ruby
score = 85
if score >= 90
  puts "A"
```

```ruby
elsif score >= 80
  puts "B"
else
  puts "C"
end
```

Loops

Loops are used to execute a block of code repeatedly. Ruby provides several types of loops, including while, until, and for.

The while Loop

The while loop executes a block of code as long as a specified condition is true.

```ruby
counter = 0
while counter < 5
  puts "Counter is #{counter}"
  counter += 1
end
```

The until Loop

The until loop is the opposite of the while loop. It executes a block of code as long as a specified condition is false.

```ruby
counter = 0
until counter == 5
  puts "Counter is #{counter}"
  counter += 1
end
```

The for Loop

The for loop is used to iterate over a range, an array, or other enumerable objects.

```ruby
for i in 1..5
  puts "Iteration #{i}"
end
```

Iterators

Ruby offers powerful iterators that simplify repetitive tasks. The each iterator is commonly used to loop through elements in an array or other enumerable objects.

```ruby
fruits = ["apple", "banana", "cherry"]
fruits.each do |fruit|
  puts "I like #{fruit}s"
end
```

Breaking and Exiting Loops

You can use the break statement to exit a loop prematurely when a specific condition is met.

```ruby
numbers = [1, 2, 3, 4, 5]
numbers.each do |number|
  break if number > 3
  puts "Number: #{number}"
end
```

Conclusion

Control flow and loops are essential tools in your Ruby programming toolkit. In this section, we explored conditional statements, including if, else, and elsif, which allow you to make decisions based on conditions. We also examined different types of loops, such as while, until, and for, which enable you to execute code repeatedly. Additionally, iterators like each make it easy to work with collections of data.

Understanding when and how to use these control structures and loops is crucial for building dynamic and responsive Ruby applications. As you continue to develop your coding skills, you'll find these concepts indispensable for solving a wide range of programming challenges.

2.4 Arrays and Hashes in Ruby

Arrays and hashes are fundamental data structures in Ruby for storing and organizing collections of data. In this section, we'll explore how to work with arrays and hashes, including creating, accessing, and manipulating them.

Arrays

An array in Ruby is an ordered collection of objects, where each object is assigned a unique index starting from 0. Arrays can store a mix of different data types, including integers, strings, or even other arrays.

Creating Arrays

You can create an array in Ruby by enclosing a list of elements in square brackets [ ].

```ruby
fruits = ["apple", "banana", "cherry"]
```

Accessing Elements

You can access individual elements of an array using their index, with the first element at index 0.

```ruby
first_fruit = fruits[0]  # "apple"
second_fruit = fruits[1] # "banana"
```

Modifying Arrays

You can add elements to an array using the << operator or the push method. To remove elements, you can use the pop method.

```
fruits << "date"        # Adds "date" to the end of the array
fruits.push("fig")      # Also adds "fig" to the end of the array
last_fruit = fruits.pop # Removes and returns the last element ("fig")
```

Hashes

A hash in Ruby is a collection of key-value pairs. Each key is unique within the hash, and you can use it to retrieve its associated value.

Creating Hashes

You can create a hash in Ruby by enclosing a list of key-value pairs within curly braces {}.

```
person = { "name" => "Alice", "age" => 30, "city" => "New York" }
```

Accessing Values

You can access the values in a hash using the keys.

```
name = person["name"]   # "Alice"
age = person["age"]     # 30
```

Modifying Hashes

You can add new key-value pairs to a hash or update existing values.

```
person["email"] = "alice@example.com" # Adds a new key-value pair
person["age"] = 31                    # Updates the value of the "age" key
```

Iterating through Arrays and Hashes

You can use iterators to loop through the elements of an array or the key-value pairs of a hash.

Iterating through an Array

The each method is commonly used to iterate through an array.

```
fruits = ["apple", "banana", "cherry"]
fruits.each do |fruit|
  puts "I like #{fruit}s"
end
```

Iterating through a Hash

You can use the each method with a block to iterate through the key-value pairs of a hash.

```
person = { "name" => "Alice", "age" => 30, "city" => "New York" }
person.each do |key, value|
  puts "#{key}: #{value}"
end
```

Conclusion

Arrays and hashes are versatile data structures that allow you to organize and manipulate collections of data in Ruby. Understanding how to create, access, and modify these structures is essential for working with data effectively in your Ruby programs. Whether you're processing lists of items or storing key-value pairs, arrays and hashes provide the building blocks for managing and organizing data in your applications.

2.5 Ruby Methods and Functions

Methods, also known as functions in other programming languages, are blocks of code that perform specific tasks or actions. In Ruby, methods allow you to encapsulate functionality, promote code reusability, and keep your code organized. In this section, we'll explore how to define and use methods in Ruby.

Defining Methods

In Ruby, you can define methods using the def keyword, followed by the method name and a block of code enclosed in end.

```
def greet(name)
  puts "Hello, #{name}!"
end
```

In the example above, we've defined a method named greet that takes one parameter name and prints a greeting.

Calling Methods

To call a method, you simply use its name followed by parentheses, passing any required arguments inside the parentheses.

```
greet("Alice") # Calls the greet method with the argument "Alice"
```

Method Parameters

Methods can accept zero or more parameters (also called arguments). Parameters allow you to pass data into a method for processing.

```
def add(a, b)
  return a + b
end
result = add(3, 5)
```

In the add method above, a and b are parameters, and the method returns the sum of a and b. When calling the method with `add(3, 5)`, it returns 8, which is then stored in the `result` variable.

Default Values for Parameters

You can specify default values for method parameters, making them optional when calling the method.

```ruby
def greet(name = "Guest")
  puts "Hello, #{name}!"
end
```

In this example, if you call `greet` without providing an argument, it will default to `"Guest"`.

Returning Values

Methods can return values using the `return` keyword. If no `return` statement is used, the method returns the value of the last evaluated expression.

```ruby
def multiply(a, b)
  return a * b
end
result = multiply(4, 7)
```

In this case, the `multiply` method returns the product of a and b, which is 28.

Scope of Variables

Variables declared within a method are typically local to that method and cannot be accessed outside of it. However, variables declared outside of a method (global variables or instance variables) can be accessed within the method.

```ruby
total = 0
def add_to_total(value)
  total += value # This will raise an error
end
```

In the example above, `total` is declared outside the method, but attempting to modify it within the method will raise an error. To access and modify such variables within methods, you can use method parameters or global variables.

Conclusion

Methods are a fundamental building block of Ruby programming. They allow you to encapsulate logic, promote code reuse, and keep your code organized and modular. Understanding how to define and use methods, pass arguments, and return values is essential for writing clean and maintainable Ruby code. As you continue your journey in Ruby development, you'll find methods to be a powerful tool for solving complex problems and building robust applications.

Chapter 3: Building Your First Rails Application

3.1 Creating a New Rails Project

Creating a new Ruby on Rails project is the first step in building web applications with Rails. In this section, we'll walk through the process of setting up a new Rails project, discussing the essential commands and project structure.

Prerequisites

Before creating a new Rails project, you need to ensure that you have Ruby and Rails installed on your development machine. You can check your Ruby version using the `ruby -v` command and your Rails version with the `rails -v` command. If they are not installed, you can install them using a package manager like gem:

```
gem install rails
```

Creating a New Rails Project

To create a new Rails project, open your terminal and navigate to the directory where you want to create the project. Use the `rails new` command followed by the desired project name:

```
rails new my_first_rails_app
```

Replace `my_first_rails_app` with your preferred project name. This command will generate a new Rails application in a directory with the same name as your project.

Project Structure

A newly created Rails project comes with a predefined directory structure that follows the MVC (Model-View-Controller) pattern. Here's a brief overview of some important directories and files:

- **app:** This directory contains the core of your application, including Models, Views, and Controllers.

- **config:** Configuration files for your application, such as database settings and route definitions, are located here.

- **db:** Database-related files, including migrations and the schema definition, can be found in this directory.

- **public:** Static files like CSS, JavaScript, and images are stored here and can be served directly by the web server.

- **Gemfile:** This file lists the gems (libraries) your application depends on. You can use the `bundle install` command to install them.

- **Rakefile:** This file contains tasks that can be executed using the `rake` command.

To start the development server and see your new Rails application in action, navigate to your project's directory and use the `rails server` command:

```
cd my_first_rails_app
rails server
```

This command will start the server, and you can access your application by opening a web browser and navigating to `http://localhost:3000`.

Conclusion

Creating a new Rails project is the first step in your journey to building web applications with Ruby on Rails. In this section, we covered the prerequisites, how to create a new Rails project, and provided an overview of the project structure. As you continue working on your Rails project, you'll explore different aspects of Rails development, including Models, Views, Controllers, and database management. Building your first Rails application is an exciting step toward becoming proficient in web development with this powerful framework.

3.2 Generating Models, Views, and Controllers

Once you've created a new Ruby on Rails project, the next step is to generate the core components of your application, including Models, Views, and Controllers. In this section, we'll explore how to use Rails generators to create these essential building blocks for your web application.

Rails Generators

Rails provides powerful generators that automate the creation of various parts of your application, saving you time and ensuring consistency in your codebase. To generate a component, you use the `rails generate` command, followed by the generator's name and options.

Generating a Model

A Model in Rails represents a table in your application's database. You can generate a Model using the `rails generate model` command. For example, to create a `User` model with attributes `name` and `email`, you can run:

```
rails generate model User name:string email:string
```

This command generates the `User` model file, migration file, and other necessary files. The migration file defines how the database table should be structured.

Generating a Controller

Controllers handle the logic of your application and serve as intermediaries between Models and Views. To generate a Controller, you can use the `rails generate controller` command. For instance, to create a `Users` Controller with actions for listing and creating users, you can run:

```
rails generate controller Users index create
```

This command generates the `Users` Controller file and the associated View files for the specified actions.

Generating a View

Views are responsible for presenting data to users. Rails generates views automatically when you create Controllers, but you can also generate them separately if needed. For example, to create a `show` view for the `User` model, you can run:

```
rails generate erb User show
```

This command generates the `show.html.erb` view file in the appropriate directory.

Running Migrations

After generating a Model, you need to run the database migration to create the corresponding table in your database. Use the `rails db:migrate` command:

```
rails db:migrate
```

This command reads the migration files in the `db/migrate` directory and applies them to the database.

Routes and Controllers

To make your application respond to specific URLs, you need to define routes in the `config/routes.rb` file. For example, to create a route for listing users, you can add the following to the `routes.rb` file:

```
get '/users', to: 'users#index'
```

This route maps the URL `/users` to the `index` action of the `Users` Controller.

Conclusion

Rails generators are powerful tools for quickly creating the basic components of your web application, including Models, Views, and Controllers. In this section, we've seen how to use generators to create these essential building blocks and how to run migrations to set up your database schema. By understanding and effectively using Rails generators, you can streamline the development process and maintain a consistent and organized codebase for your Ruby on Rails application.

3.3 Configuring Routes

Configuring routes is a crucial aspect of building a Ruby on Rails application. Routes determine how your application responds to HTTP requests by mapping URLs to Controller actions. In this section, we'll explore how to configure routes in a Rails application.

The `config/routes.rb` File

Routes in a Rails application are defined in the `config/routes.rb` file. This file serves as the central location for specifying the mapping between URLs and Controller actions.

Basic Route Configuration

To create a basic route, you can use the `get`, `post`, `put`, or `delete` methods in the `routes.rb` file. Here's an example of defining a route for the homepage:

```
# config/routes.rb
get '/', to: 'home#index'
```

In the above code, we use the `get` method to map the root URL `'/'` to the `index` action of the `HomeController`. When a user visits the root URL of your application, Rails will invoke the `index` action.

Route Parameters

Routes can include parameters that capture dynamic parts of the URL. For example, to create a route for displaying a user's profile with a variable `:id`, you can use the following:

```
# config/routes.rb
get '/users/:id', to: 'users#show'
```

In this case, when a user visits a URL like `/users/1`, Rails will capture the value 1 as the `:id` parameter and pass it to the `show` action of the `UsersController`.

Named Routes

Named routes provide a way to reference routes by a symbolic name rather than the URL path. This can be helpful for keeping your code DRY (Don't Repeat Yourself) and avoiding hardcoding URLs in your views. Here's an example of creating a named route:

```
# config/routes.rb
get '/contact', to: 'pages#contact', as: 'contact'
```

With the `as: 'contact'` option, you can now refer to this route in your views or controllers as `contact_path` or `contact_url`.

Resourceful Routing

In Rails, you can define routes for CRUD (Create, Read, Update, Delete) operations on resources using the `resources` method. For example, to define routes for a `Post` resource, you can use:

```ruby
# config/routes.rb
resources :posts
```

This single line generates routes for actions like `index`, `show`, `new`, `create`, `edit`, `update`, and `destroy`, mapping them to the appropriate Controller actions.

Route Constraints

Rails allows you to constrain routes based on conditions, such as the HTTP method, request format, or custom logic. For instance, to create a route that responds only to `GET` requests, you can do:

```ruby
# config/routes.rb
get '/public', to: 'pages#public', constraints: { method: 'GET' }
```

In this example, the `constraints` option ensures that the route only matches `GET` requests.

Conclusion

Configuring routes is a fundamental part of developing Ruby on Rails applications. In this section, we've explored how to define routes in the `config/routes.rb` file, create basic routes, handle route parameters, use named routes for better maintainability, and define resourceful routes for CRUD operations. By mastering route configuration, you can effectively map URLs to Controller actions, enabling your application to respond to user requests and deliver dynamic web content.

3.4 Working with Databases in Rails

Working with databases is a fundamental part of building web applications, and Ruby on Rails makes it relatively straightforward with its built-in support for databases. In this section, we'll explore how Rails handles database operations, including creating tables, defining models, and using migrations.

Database Configuration

Rails applications typically use a relational database like MySQL, PostgreSQL, or SQLite. Database configuration is specified in the `config/database.yml` file, where you can set up different configurations for development, test, and production environments.

Here's an example configuration for SQLite:

```
development:
  adapter: sqlite3
  database: db/development.sqlite3
```

Creating a Model

In Rails, a Model is an object that represents a table in your database. Models are created using Rails generators, as we discussed earlier. For instance, to create a User model, you can run:

```
rails generate model User name:string email:string
```

This command generates a model file, a migration file, and other necessary files. The migration file defines how the users table should be structured.

Running Migrations

Migrations are scripts that define changes to your database schema. To create the corresponding table in the database, you need to run the migrations. Use the rails db:migrate command:

```
rails db:migrate
```

This command reads the migration files in the db/migrate directory and applies them to the database. It also keeps track of which migrations have been run, so you can easily update your database schema as your application evolves.

Interacting with the Database

Rails provides an Object-Relational Mapping (ORM) framework called Active Record, which allows you to interact with the database using Ruby objects. You can perform operations like creating, reading, updating, and deleting records without writing raw SQL queries.

For example, to create a new User record, you can do:

```
user = User.new(name: "Alice", email: "alice@example.com")
user.save
```

To find users with a specific condition, you can use methods like where:

```
users = User.where(name: "Alice")
```

Seeding the Database

During development and testing, it's common to populate your database with initial data for testing purposes. Rails provides a way to seed the database using a file called db/seeds.rb. You can define data creation logic in this file and then run:

```
rails db:seed
```

Database Queries

Active Record allows you to build complex database queries using a Ruby DSL. For example, to find all users whose names contain "John" and are older than 25, you can write:

```
users = User.where("name LIKE ? AND age > ?", "%John%", 25)
```

This will generate the appropriate SQL query to fetch the desired records.

Conclusion

Working with databases in Ruby on Rails is made convenient with its built-in features for defining models, running migrations, and interacting with the database using Active Record. In this section, we've explored how Rails handles database operations, from configuring the database connection to creating models, running migrations, and querying the database. As you build your Rails application, you'll find that this database integration simplifies the process of persisting and retrieving data, allowing you to focus more on your application's logic and functionality.

3.5 Adding Basic Styling with CSS

User interfaces play a significant role in the success of web applications, and one crucial aspect of a polished UI is styling. In this section, we'll explore how to add basic styling to your Ruby on Rails application using CSS (Cascading Style Sheets).

CSS in Rails

Ruby on Rails doesn't dictate how you should manage your CSS, leaving the choice of CSS organization up to you. However, it provides a few conventions and tools to help you structure your stylesheets effectively.

Asset Pipeline

Rails utilizes the Asset Pipeline to manage and serve assets like stylesheets, JavaScript files, and images. The Asset Pipeline preprocesses and compiles your assets to minimize load times. Stylesheets are typically stored in the `app/assets/stylesheets` directory.

Application.css (or Application.scss)

By default, Rails includes an `application.css` (or `application.scss` for SCSS) file, which serves as the entry point for your application's styles. It's recommended to use this file for including other stylesheets and organizing your global styles.

Adding Custom Styles

To add custom styles to your Rails application, you can create a new CSS file in the `app/assets/stylesheets` directory or add your styles to the `application.css` (or `application.scss`) file. Here's an example of creating a `custom.css` file:

```
touch app/assets/stylesheets/custom.css
```

Inside your `custom.css` file, you can define CSS rules to style specific elements or classes on your web pages. For instance, to style all headings with a blue color, you can write:

```
/* app/assets/stylesheets/custom.css */
h1, h2, h3, h4, h5, h6 {
  color: blue;
}
```

Asset Pipeline Directives

To include your custom styles in your application layout, you can use the `stylesheet_link_tag` helper method in the `<head>` section of your layout file (usually `app/views/layouts/application.html.erb`). Here's an example:

```
<!-- app/views/layouts/application.html.erb -->
<!DOCTYPE html>
<html>
  <head>
    <!-- ... other head content ... -->
    <%= stylesheet_link_tag 'application', 'custom' %>
  </head>
  <body>
    <!-- ... body content ... -->
  </body>
</html>
```

In the code above, we're including both the `application.css` (for global styles) and our custom `custom.css` stylesheet.

CSS Frameworks

While you can create your styles from scratch, many developers prefer using CSS frameworks like Bootstrap, Foundation, or Bulma to streamline the styling process. Rails makes it easy to integrate these frameworks into your application.

To include a CSS framework, you typically add its CSS and JavaScript files to your assets and follow the framework's documentation for usage instructions.

Conclusion

Adding basic styling to your Ruby on Rails application is an essential step in creating an appealing and user-friendly interface. Rails provides a structured way to manage CSS using the Asset Pipeline, and you can customize your stylesheets to match your application's design. Whether you're writing your styles from scratch or using a CSS framework, effective styling enhances the user experience and contributes to the overall success of your web application.

Chapter 4: Working with Models and Databases

4.1 Understanding Active Record

Active Record is a crucial component of Ruby on Rails, responsible for interacting with your database in an object-oriented manner. It provides an abstraction layer that allows you to work with your database using Ruby objects, making database operations more straightforward and intuitive.

The Active Record Pattern

Active Record is based on the Active Record pattern, which is part of the Model layer in the MVC (Model-View-Controller) architecture. In Rails, Models are Ruby classes that inherit from `ActiveRecord::Base`, and each Model class represents a table in your database.

For example, if you have a `User` Model, you can use it to interact with the `users` table in your database. Here's a basic example of a `User` Model:

```
class User < ActiveRecord::Base
end
```

With this simple declaration, you gain the ability to create, read, update, and delete records in the `users` table using Ruby code.

CRUD Operations with Active Record

Active Record simplifies CRUD (Create, Read, Update, Delete) operations by providing intuitive methods for each action:

- **Create:** You can create a new record in the database by creating a new instance of the Model and calling `save` on it.

  ```
  user = User.new(name: "Alice", email: "alice@example.com")
  user.save
  ```

- **Read:** To retrieve records from the database, you can use methods like `find`, `all`, `where`, and more.

  ```
  user = User.find(1) # Find a user with ID 1
  users = User.all # Retrieve all users
  users = User.where(name: "Alice") # Find users with a specific conditio
  n
  ```

- **Update:** To update a record, you can first find it and then modify its attributes before calling `save`.

  ```
  user = User.find(1)
  user.name = "Bob"
  user.save
  ```

- **Delete:** To delete a record, you can call the `destroy` method on an instance.

```
user = User.find(1)
user.destroy
```

Active Record Associations

Active Record also simplifies working with associations between Models, such as one-to-many and many-to-many relationships. You can define associations using methods like `has_many`, `belongs_to`, and `has_and_belongs_to_many`.

For example, if you have a `Post` Model and a `Comment` Model, you can define a one-to-many association like this:

```
class Post < ActiveRecord::Base
  has_many :comments
end

class Comment < ActiveRecord::Base
  belongs_to :post
end
```

With these associations, you can easily access related records and navigate the database structure.

Migrations and Database Schema

Active Record works in harmony with database migrations to define and modify the database schema. Migrations allow you to make changes to your database in a versioned and reversible way. You can create, modify, or drop database tables, columns, and indexes using migrations.

Conclusion

Active Record is a fundamental part of Ruby on Rails, providing a powerful and intuitive way to interact with your database. It simplifies CRUD operations, allows you to define associations between Models, and works seamlessly with database migrations. Understanding how to use Active Record effectively is essential for building robust and data-driven web applications with Ruby on Rails.

4.2 Creating and Migrating Databases

Creating and migrating databases is a crucial aspect of Ruby on Rails development. In this section, we'll explore how to create a new database, define its structure, and perform migrations to modify the database schema.

Database Configuration

In a Rails application, database configuration is defined in the `config/database.yml` file. This file specifies the database adapter, database name, host, username, and password for different environments (e.g., development, test, production). By default, Rails uses SQLite in development and testing environments, but you can configure it to use other databases like MySQL or PostgreSQL.

Here's an example database configuration for PostgreSQL:

```
development:
  adapter: postgresql
  encoding: unicode
  database: myapp_development
  pool: 5
  username: myapp
  password: secret
  host: localhost
```

Creating a New Database

Before you can work with a database, you need to create it. Rails provides a convenient command to create a new database based on the configuration in `database.yml`. Use the following command:

```
rails db:create
```

This command will create a new database with the name specified in your configuration file (e.g., `myapp_development` in the example above).

Database Migrations

Database migrations in Rails are scripts that define changes to your database schema. Migrations allow you to make changes to your database in a structured and versioned manner. Each migration file is timestamped and contains instructions for creating or modifying database tables, columns, indexes, and more.

To generate a new migration, you can use the `rails generate migration` command followed by a descriptive name. For example, to create a migration to add a `username` column to the `users` table, you can run:

```
rails generate migration AddUsernameToUsers username:string
```

This command generates a new migration file in the `db/migrate` directory. You can then open the migration file and define the changes you want to make to the database schema.

Defining Database Changes

Inside a migration file, you use Ruby code to specify database changes. For example, to add the `username` column to the `users` table, you can modify the migration like this:

```
class AddUsernameToUsers < ActiveRecord::Migration[6.0]
  def change
    add_column :users, :username, :string
  end
end
```

In this example, we use the add_column method to specify that we're adding a username column of type string to the users table.

Running Migrations

To apply a migration and update the database schema, you can use the rails db:migrate command:

```
rails db:migrate
```

This command will execute all pending migrations in the order they were created. Rails keeps track of which migrations have been applied, so you can safely roll back or reapply migrations as needed.

Rollback and Redo

If you need to undo a migration, you can use the rails db:rollback command. For example, to undo the last migration, you can run:

```
rails db:rollback
```

You can also use the rails db:migrate:status command to see the status of migrations and check which migrations have been applied.

Additionally, Rails provides the rails db:migrate:redo command, which rolls back the last migration and then reapplies it. This can be useful for quickly testing migrations.

Conclusion

Creating and migrating databases is an essential part of Ruby on Rails development. In this section, we've covered how to configure your database in database.yml, create a new database, generate and define migrations, and perform database schema changes using migrations. Understanding how to work with migrations and maintain a structured database schema is crucial for building and evolving your Rails application.

4.3 Defining Models and Associations

In Ruby on Rails, Models are the representation of database tables and the primary way to interact with data. In this section, we'll dive into defining Models and establishing associations between them, which is essential for building complex database-driven applications.

Creating a Model

To create a Model in Rails, you can use the `rails generate model` command followed by the name of the Model and its attributes. For example, to create a `User` Model with `name` and `email` attributes, you can run:

```
rails generate model User name:string email:string
```

This command generates a Model file (e.g., `user.rb`) in the `app/models` directory and a migration file (e.g., `20231002123456_create_users.rb`) in the `db/migrate` directory. The migration file defines how the corresponding database table should be structured.

Defining Model Associations

Rails provides a straightforward way to define associations between Models. Associations allow you to represent relationships between database tables, such as one-to-many, many-to-one, and many-to-many relationships. Here are some common types of associations:

1. One-to-Many

A one-to-many association represents a relationship where one record in the Model is associated with many records in another Model. For example, a `User` Model can have many `Post` records. To define this association, you can do the following:

```ruby
class User < ApplicationRecord
  has_many :posts
end

class Post < ApplicationRecord
  belongs_to :user
end
```

In this example, the `User` Model uses `has_many :posts`, and the `Post` Model uses `belongs_to :user`.

2. Many-to-One (Inverse of One-to-Many)

The inverse of a one-to-many association is a many-to-one association. In the example above, the `Post` Model has a many-to-one association with the `User` Model. This means that each `Post` belongs to one `User`. The `belongs_to` method is used to define this association.

3. Many-to-Many

Many-to-many associations are used when multiple records in one Model can be associated with multiple records in another Model. For example, a `User` can have many `Role` records, and each `Role` can belong to many `User` records. To define this association, you can use the `has_and_belongs_to_many` method:

```ruby
class User < ApplicationRecord
  has_and_belongs_to_many :roles
end
```

```
class Role < ApplicationRecord
  has_and_belongs_to_many :users
end
```

In this example, a join table is needed in the database to store the associations between User and Role records.

Customizing Associations

Rails provides various options and customization options for associations. For example, you can specify the foreign key, class name, dependent behavior (e.g., :destroy, :nullify), and more in your association definitions to tailor them to your application's needs.

Database Migrations for Associations

After defining associations, you may need to update your database schema to reflect these associations. This can be done using database migrations. For example, if you've added an association between User and Post, you may need to create a migration to add a user_id column to the posts table.

Conclusion

Defining Models and establishing associations between them is fundamental to building robust and data-driven Ruby on Rails applications. By properly defining Models and their relationships, you can ensure that your application's data is structured and organized efficiently, enabling you to perform complex queries and operations with ease. Understanding how to use Rails' built-in association methods and customization options is essential for effective database modeling in your Rails project.

4.4 Querying the Database

In Ruby on Rails, querying the database is a common task when you need to retrieve and manipulate data. Rails provides a powerful querying interface through Active Record, allowing you to perform complex database queries with ease. In this section, we'll explore various querying techniques and methods.

Basic Querying

The simplest way to retrieve records from the database is by using methods provided by Active Record. For example, to retrieve all User records from the database, you can use the all method:

```
users = User.all
```

This will fetch all the records from the users table and store them in the users variable as an array of User objects.

Conditions and Filtering

Often, you'll want to filter records based on specific conditions. Active Record provides the `where` method for this purpose. For example, to find all `User` records with the name "Alice," you can do:

```
users = User.where(name: "Alice")
```

You can also use various comparison operators in conditions. For instance, to find users older than 25:

```
users = User.where("age > ?", 25)
```

The `?` placeholder is used to safely interpolate user-provided values into SQL queries, preventing SQL injection.

Chaining Queries

Active Record allows you to chain multiple query methods together to create more complex queries. For example, you can chain `where` and `order` to find users named "Alice" and order them by their age:

```
users = User.where(name: "Alice").order(:age)
```

This will first filter the users with the name "Alice" and then order the results by age in ascending order.

Selecting Specific Columns

By default, Active Record retrieves all columns of a table when querying. However, you can limit the columns retrieved by using the `select` method. For example, to retrieve only the names of users named "Alice":

```
names = User.where(name: "Alice").select(:name)
```

This will fetch only the `name` column, and the result will be an array of `User` objects with only the `name` attribute loaded.

Aggregations

Active Record provides methods for aggregating data, such as `count`, `sum`, `average`, and `maximum`. For example, to count the number of users:

```
count = User.count
```

Or to find the average age of users:

```
average_age = User.average(:age)
```

Using SQL Fragments

In some cases, you may need to write custom SQL queries. Active Record allows you to include SQL fragments in your queries using the `find_by_sql` method. For example:

```
results = User.find_by_sql("SELECT * FROM users WHERE age > 25")
```

While using SQL fragments should be done with caution, it can be useful for complex queries that cannot be expressed easily with the standard Active Record query methods.

Conclusion

Querying the database is a fundamental part of building Ruby on Rails applications. Active Record simplifies the process by providing a rich set of query methods for filtering, sorting, aggregating, and retrieving data from the database. By mastering these querying techniques, you can efficiently work with data and build feature-rich applications with Rails.

4.5 Validations and Callbacks in Rails Models

When working with Ruby on Rails Models, ensuring data integrity and executing specific actions during object lifecycle events are critical. In this section, we'll delve into the concepts of validations and callbacks, which help maintain the quality of data and perform actions at the right moments.

Validations

Validations are rules that you define in your Model classes to ensure that the data being saved into the database meets specific criteria. Rails provides a wide range of built-in validation helpers to check attributes for correctness.

For instance, to validate the presence of a `name` attribute in the `User` Model, you can do:

```
class User < ApplicationRecord
  validates :name, presence: true
end
```

This ensures that a `User` record cannot be saved without a `name` value. Similarly, you can validate attributes for uniqueness, length, format, and more.

```
class User < ApplicationRecord
  validates :email, uniqueness: true
  validates :password, length: { minimum: 6 }
  validates :username, format: { with: /\A[a-zA-Z0-9]+\z/ }
end
```

If a validation fails, Rails won't save the object to the database and provides error messages that can be used to inform the user of the issue.

Callbacks

Callbacks are methods that get executed at specific points in the lifecycle of an object. They allow you to add custom logic before or after certain events, such as object creation, saving, or deletion.

Rails Models provide a variety of callback methods that you can use. Here are some common ones:

- before_validation: Runs before validation checks.
- after_validation: Runs after validation checks.
- before_save: Runs just before an object is saved.
- after_save: Runs after an object is successfully saved.
- before_create: Runs just before a new object is created.
- after_create: Runs after a new object is created.
- before_update: Runs just before an object is updated.
- after_update: Runs after an object is updated.
- before_destroy: Runs just before an object is destroyed.
- after_destroy: Runs after an object is destroyed.

For example, you can use before_save to automatically capitalize the name attribute before saving it to the database:

```ruby
class User < ApplicationRecord
  before_save :capitalize_name

  private

  def capitalize_name
    self.name = name.capitalize
  end
end
```

Callbacks provide a way to encapsulate logic related to specific object events and are commonly used to enforce business rules, trigger notifications, or perform related tasks when certain actions occur.

Custom Validations and Callbacks

In addition to built-in validations and callbacks, you can define custom ones to suit your application's needs. Custom validations and callbacks are implemented as methods in your Model class.

For instance, to create a custom validation to ensure that a User record's birthdate is in the past, you can do:

```ruby
class User < ApplicationRecord
  validate :birthdate_in_past
```

```ruby
  private

  def birthdate_in_past
    if birthdate.present? && birthdate > Date.today
      errors.add(:birthdate, "must be in the past")
    end
  end
end
```

Here, we define a custom validation method called `birthdate_in_past`, which checks if the `birthdate` attribute is in the future and adds an error message if it is.

Similarly, you can define custom callback methods to perform specific actions at different points in the object's lifecycle.

Conclusion

Validations and callbacks are powerful tools in Ruby on Rails Models, enabling you to maintain data integrity, enforce business rules, and trigger actions at specific events in an object's lifecycle. By understanding and using these concepts effectively, you can create robust and reliable Rails applications that ensure data quality and perform tasks seamlessly throughout the application's lifecycle.

Chapter 5: Crafting Beautiful Views with ERB and HAML

5.1 Introduction to Views in Rails

In Ruby on Rails, views are responsible for rendering the HTML that is sent to the client's web browser. Views are a critical part of the MVC (Model-View-Controller) architecture and are responsible for presenting data to the user in a human-readable format. In this section, we'll explore the fundamentals of views in Rails and introduce you to two popular templating engines: ERB (Embedded Ruby) and HAML (HTML Abstraction Markup Language).

Understanding Views

Views in Rails are typically located in the app/views directory, organized into subdirectories corresponding to the controllers they are associated with. For example, if you have a PostsController, its views would be located in the app/views/posts directory.

Each action in a controller can have a corresponding view with the same name as the action. For instance, the index action in the PostsController would have a corresponding index.html.erb (or index.html.haml) view file.

ERB (Embedded Ruby)

ERB is the default templating engine in Ruby on Rails. It allows you to embed Ruby code directly into your HTML templates. This enables dynamic generation of HTML content based on data from the controller or the Model layer.

Here's a simple example of an ERB template:

```
<!DOCTYPE html>
<html>
<head>
  <title>Welcome to My Blog</title>
</head>
<body>
  <h1>Welcome to My Blog</h1>
  <ul>
    <% @posts.each do |post| %>
      <li><%= post.title %></li>
    <% end %>
  </ul>
</body>
</html>
```

In this example, you can see that Ruby code is enclosed within <% %> tags, and the output to be included in the HTML is enclosed within <%= %> tags. This allows you to embed dynamic data from the controller into your views.

HAML is an alternative templating engine that is often used in Rails applications. It offers a more concise and visually appealing way to write HTML templates. Instead of using tags, HAML uses indentation to define the structure of HTML elements.

Here's the same example as above, written in HAML:

```
!!!
%html
  %head
    %title Welcome to My Blog
  %body
    %h1 Welcome to My Blog
    %ul
      - @posts.each do |post|
        %li= post.title
```

In HAML, indentation is crucial for defining the hierarchy of elements. The use of hyphens (-) and = for code and output respectively is also a distinguishing feature.

Choosing Between ERB and HAML

The choice between ERB and HAML is a matter of personal preference and project requirements. ERB is the default and widely used, while HAML offers a more concise syntax. It's essential to consider factors like your team's familiarity with a particular templating engine and the readability of the code.

Conclusion

Views play a crucial role in Ruby on Rails applications by presenting data to users in a human-readable format. ERB and HAML are two popular templating engines that allow you to create dynamic and visually appealing views. Understanding how to work with views and choose the appropriate templating engine for your project is essential for building user-friendly web applications with Rails.

5.2 Using ERB for Template Rendering

In Ruby on Rails, ERB (Embedded Ruby) is the default templating engine used for rendering views. ERB allows you to embed Ruby code within HTML templates, enabling dynamic content generation. In this section, we'll explore the usage of ERB for template rendering in Rails views.

ERB Syntax

ERB uses specific syntax to embed Ruby code within HTML templates. There are two main types of ERB tags:

- `<% %>`: These tags are used to embed Ruby code that is evaluated but does not produce any output in the final HTML. For example, you can use `<% %>` tags for control flow statements and assignments.

```
<% if @user.logged_in? %>
  <p>Welcome, <%= @user.name %></p>
<% else %>
  <p>Please log in</p>
<% end %>
```

- `<%= %>`: These tags are used to embed Ruby code that is evaluated and produces output in the final HTML. This is commonly used for displaying dynamic content.

```
<p>User's email: <%= @user.email %></p>
```

Accessing Controller Data

In a Rails view, you have access to instance variables defined in the corresponding controller action. For example, if you have a `@user` instance variable in your `UsersController`, you can use it in the view:

```
<p>User's name: <%= @user.name %></p>
```

This allows you to pass data from the controller to the view and render it dynamically.

Rendering Partial Views

ERB also supports rendering partial views, which are reusable templates that can be included in other views. You can render a partial view using the `render` method. For example, to render a partial named `_post.html.erb`, you can use:

```
<%= render 'post', post: @post %>
```

This will render the `_post.html.erb` partial and pass the `@post` variable to it.

Layouts and Yield

In Rails, you can define layout templates that provide a common structure for your views. Layouts are typically used for headers, footers, and navigation menus that are shared across multiple pages. You can specify a layout in your controller:

```
class PostsController < ApplicationController
  layout 'application'
  # ...
end
```

Within a layout, you can use the `yield` method to indicate where the content of the specific view should be inserted. For example:

```
<!DOCTYPE html>
<html>
<head>
```

```
    <title>My Blog</title>
  </head>
  <body>
    <header>
      <h1>My Blog</h1>
      <nav>
        <!-- Navigation links go here -->
      </nav>
    </header>

    <main>
      <%= yield %>
    </main>

    <footer>
      <!-- Footer content goes here -->
    </footer>
  </body>
</html>
```

The content from the view will replace the `<%= yield %>` tag in the layout.

Conclusion

ERB is a powerful and widely used templating engine in Ruby on Rails, allowing you to create dynamic views by embedding Ruby code within HTML templates. Understanding how to use ERB tags, access controller data, render partial views, and define layouts is essential for crafting visually appealing and functional web applications in Rails.

5.3 Simplifying Views with HAML

In Ruby on Rails, views play a crucial role in presenting data to users. While the default templating engine is ERB (Embedded Ruby), Rails also supports alternative engines like HAML (HTML Abstraction Markup Language). HAML offers a concise and visually appealing syntax for creating HTML templates. In this section, we'll explore the usage of HAML to simplify views in Rails.

Installing HAML

Before using HAML in your Rails application, you need to add it to your project's Gemfile and run the bundle install command:

```
# Gemfile
gem 'haml'
```

After installing the gem, your Rails application will be able to recognize `.html.haml` files as valid view templates.

HAML uses indentation to define the structure of HTML elements, making it more concise and readable than traditional HTML. Here's a brief overview of HAML syntax:

- Elements: To define an HTML element, start a new line with the element name, followed by optional attributes and content. Elements are indented to indicate nesting.

```
%div
    %p This is a paragraph.
    %a(href="#") Click here
```

- Attributes: Attributes can be defined within parentheses after the element name. Multiple attributes are separated by spaces.

```
%a(href="#", class="btn btn-primary") Click me
```

- Content: Text content can be placed directly after the element name, followed by a pipe (|) character.

```
%h1 My Blog
| Welcome to my blog!
```

- Classes and IDs: To specify classes and IDs, use .class-name and #id-name notation.

```
%div.container
    %ul#nav-list
        %li.menu-item Home
        %li.menu-item About
```

Interpolating Ruby Code

Just like in ERB, you can embed Ruby code within HAML templates using the = symbol. This allows you to evaluate and include dynamic content.

```
%h1= @post.title
%p= "Published on #{l(@post.published_at, format: :long)}"
```

Conditional Statements and Loops

HAML supports Ruby's control flow constructs like if, else, unless, and each. These can be used to conditionally render elements or iterate over collections.

```
- if @user.logged_in?
  %p Welcome, #{@user.name}!
- else
  %p Please log in.

%ul
  - @posts.each do |post|
    %li= post.title
```

Partial Views in HAML

Rendering partial views in HAML is similar to ERB. You can use the render method to include a partial in your template.

```
= render 'shared/header'
```

Advantages of HAML

HAML's concise and indentation-based syntax can lead to cleaner and more readable views. It encourages consistent formatting and eliminates the need for closing tags, reducing the chances of syntax errors.

However, the choice between ERB and HAML often depends on personal preference and team familiarity. It's essential to consider your project's requirements and your team's comfort when choosing a templating engine.

Conclusion

HAML is a valuable alternative to ERB in Ruby on Rails, offering a more concise and visually appealing syntax for creating views. Understanding HAML's syntax, embedding Ruby code, using control flow constructs, and rendering partial views can simplify your view templates and lead to cleaner and more maintainable code in your Rails application.

5.4 Layouts and Partials

In Ruby on Rails, views play a crucial role in presenting web pages to users. Views can become complex, especially in applications with multiple pages or shared components like headers and footers. To maintain code organization and reusability, Rails provides layouts and partials as powerful tools. In this section, we'll delve into layouts and partials in Rails views.

Layouts

Layouts are templates that provide a common structure for your views. They are typically used for elements that appear on multiple pages, such as headers, footers, and navigation menus. By using layouts, you can ensure a consistent look and feel across your application.

To specify a layout for a controller, you can set the layout option in the controller:

```
class ApplicationController < ActionController::Base
  layout 'application' # This specifies the 'application.html.erb' layout as
the default.
end
```

You can also specify a layout for a specific action within the controller:

```
class PostsController < ApplicationController
  layout 'blog', only: [:index, :show]
```

```
  layout 'admin', except: [:index, :show]
end
```

Layouts typically have a .html.erb file extension and are located in the app/views/layouts directory. Here's an example of a simple layout:

```erb
<!DOCTYPE html>
<html>
<head>
  <title>My Blog</title>
</head>
<body>
  <%= render 'shared/header' %>

  <main>
    <%= yield %>
  </main>

  <%= render 'shared/footer' %>
</body>
</html>
```

In this layout, the yield method is used to define where the content of the specific view will be inserted.

Partials

Partials are reusable view fragments that can be included in multiple views or layouts. They help in keeping your views DRY (Don't Repeat Yourself) by reducing duplication of code for common components.

To create a partial, you typically use an underscore _ prefix in the filename, like _header.html.erb. Then, you can render the partial in a view or layout using the render method:

```erb
<%= render 'shared/header' %>
```

Partials can also accept local variables, allowing you to pass data to them. For example:

```erb
<%= render 'shared/comment', comment: @comment %>
```

In this case, the @comment variable is passed to the _comment.html.erb partial as a local variable.

Nested Partials

Partials can be nested within other partials, providing a way to create complex, reusable components. For example, you might have a _post.html.erb partial that includes a _comments.html.erb partial:

```
<!-- _post.html.erb -->
<article class="post">
  <h2><%= post.title %></h2>
  <div class="post-content">
    <%= post.content %>
  </div>
  <%= render 'shared/comments', comments: post.comments %>
</article>
```

In this example, the _comments.html.erb partial is used to render comments for a post within the post's partial.

Conclusion

Layouts and partials are essential tools in Ruby on Rails for maintaining code organization, reusability, and a consistent user interface. By using layouts, you can define the overall structure of your application's pages, and by using partials, you can create reusable components that help keep your views DRY. These techniques are valuable for building maintainable and user-friendly web applications.

5.5 Working with Forms and Form Helpers

In web applications, forms are a fundamental component for user interaction. Ruby on Rails provides powerful tools and form helpers to simplify the process of creating and processing forms in your application. In this section, we'll explore working with forms and form helpers in Rails.

Creating Forms

To create a form in Rails, you can use the form_with helper method, which is designed to simplify form creation and submission. Here's a basic example of creating a form to submit user data:

```
<%= form_with(model: @user, url: users_path) do |form| %>
  <%= form.label :username %>
  <%= form.text_field :username %>

  <%= form.label :email %>
  <%= form.email_field :email %>

  <%= form.submit 'Submit' %>
<% end %>
```

In this example, we use the form_with helper and specify the model (in this case, @user) and the URL to which the form data should be submitted.

Form Fields

Rails provides various form field helpers to create input fields for different data types. For example, you can use `text_field` for text input, `password_field` for passwords, `email_field` for email addresses, and more. These helpers generate HTML input elements with appropriate attributes and names for easy processing on the server.

Strong Parameters

When processing form submissions in Rails, it's essential to use strong parameters to whitelist the parameters that can be updated. In your controller, you can define a private method to permit specific attributes for mass assignment:

```ruby
def user_params
  params.require(:user).permit(:username, :email)
end
```

This helps protect your application from mass-assignment vulnerabilities.

Handling Form Submissions

In your controller, you can handle form submissions in the corresponding action. For example, if your form is submitted to the `create` action of the `UsersController`, you can create a new user like this:

```ruby
def create
  @user = User.new(user_params)
  if @user.save
    redirect_to @user
  else
    render 'new'
  end
end
```

If the user is successfully created, we redirect to the user's show page; otherwise, we render the new view again to display validation errors.

Form Validation

Rails provides built-in support for form validation using ActiveRecord validations. If a model has validation errors, Rails will automatically add error messages to the form fields when you render the form again. For example:

```erb
<%= form_with(model: @user, url: users_path) do |form| %>
  <%= form.label :username %>
  <%= form.text_field :username %>
  <%= form.error_message :username %>

  <%= form.label :email %>
  <%= form.email_field :email %>
  <%= form.error_message :email %>
```

```
  <%= form.submit 'Submit' %>
<% end %>
```

In this example, `form.error_message` is used to display validation errors next to the corresponding input fields.

Complex Forms

Rails can handle complex forms involving associations between models. You can use fields like `fields_for` to handle nested forms for associated models. This is useful when you need to create or update records for multiple models in a single form submission.

Conclusion

Working with forms and form helpers is a fundamental part of web application development, and Rails makes it easier with its form helper methods and conventions. By following Rails' conventions for form creation, handling submissions, and incorporating validation, you can build robust and user-friendly forms in your Ruby on Rails applications.

Chapter 6: Mastering Controllers and Routes

6.1 The Role of Controllers in Rails

Controllers play a crucial role in the Ruby on Rails framework. They act as intermediaries between the application's models and views, handling incoming HTTP requests, processing data, and rendering views to provide responses. In this section, we'll dive into the role of controllers in Rails and how they fit into the MVC (Model-View-Controller) architecture.

The MVC Architecture Recap

Before delving into controllers, let's briefly recap the MVC architecture in Rails. MVC is a design pattern that separates an application into three interconnected components:

1. **Model**: The model represents the application's data and business logic. It interacts with the database, retrieves and stores data, and defines the relationships between different data entities. In Rails, models are typically ActiveRecord classes.

2. **View**: The view is responsible for rendering the user interface and presenting data to the user. It's where you define the HTML templates that are sent to the client's browser. Views are often written using embedded Ruby (ERB) or other templating languages.

3. **Controller**: The controller acts as an intermediary between the model and view. It receives HTTP requests from clients, processes them, interacts with the model to retrieve or manipulate data, and then renders the appropriate view as a response. Controllers are responsible for handling the application's business logic and flow.

Creating Controllers

In Rails, controllers are typically placed in the app/controllers directory and are named after the resources they manage. For example, if you're building a blog application, you might have a PostsController to handle blog post-related actions.

To generate a controller, you can use Rails' generator tool. For instance, to create a PostsController, you can run:

```
rails generate controller Posts
```

This generates the PostsController class along with several default actions like index, show, new, edit, create, update, and destroy. These actions correspond to common CRUD (Create, Read, Update, Delete) operations for resources.

Actions and Routes

Each action in a controller corresponds to a specific HTTP request, typically one of the following:

- **GET**: Used for retrieving data.
- **POST**: Used for creating new records.
- **PUT/PATCH**: Used for updating existing records.
- **DELETE**: Used for deleting records.

Rails routes incoming requests to the appropriate controller action based on the request's HTTP method and URL. This routing is defined in the config/routes.rb file. For example:

```ruby
# config/routes.rb
resources :posts
```

This single line of code generates routes for the PostsController, mapping HTTP requests to actions like index, show, new, create, edit, update, and destroy.

Controller Actions

Controller actions are Ruby methods defined within the controller class. They perform specific tasks based on the received HTTP request. For example, an index action might retrieve a list of records to display on a page, while a create action might save a new record to the database.

Here's a simplified example of a PostsController with index and show actions:

```ruby
class PostsController < ApplicationController
  def index
    @posts = Post.all
  end

  def show
    @post = Post.find(params[:id])
  end
end
```

In the index action, we retrieve all posts from the database and store them in the @posts instance variable, which can be used in the corresponding view. In the show action, we find a specific post based on the :id parameter from the URL.

Rendering Views

Controllers are responsible for rendering views, and Rails makes this process straightforward. By convention, views are stored in the app/views directory within subdirectories corresponding to the controller and action. For example, the view for the show action of the PostsController would be located at app/views/posts/show.html.erb.

To render a view from a controller action, you typically use the render method:

```ruby
def show
  @post = Post.find(params[:id])
  render :show
end
```

In this example, we're rendering the `show.html.erb` view, which corresponds to the `show` action.

Controllers are central to the request-response cycle in Ruby on Rails applications. They receive incoming requests, process data, interact with models, and render views to provide a complete response to the client. Understanding the role of controllers and how they interact with models and views is fundamental to building robust and efficient Rails applications.

6.2 Handling HTTP Requests

In the previous section, we discussed the role of controllers in Ruby on Rails applications. Now, let's dive deeper into how controllers handle incoming HTTP requests, including routing and request parameters.

Routing in Rails

Routing is the process of determining which controller action should handle an incoming HTTP request based on the request's URL and HTTP method. In Rails, the routing configuration is defined in the `config/routes.rb` file.

Let's say you have a blog application, and you want to handle requests for viewing a list of posts and viewing a single post. You can define routes for these actions like this:

```ruby
# config/routes.rb
get '/posts', to: 'posts#index'
get '/posts/:id', to: 'posts#show', as: 'post'
```

In this example, we've defined two routes:

1. The first route maps a GET request to the URL path /posts to the `index` action of the `PostsController`. This action typically displays a list of all posts.

2. The second route maps a GET request to URLs like /posts/1 or /posts/42 to the `show` action of the `PostsController`. The `:id` segment in the URL is a placeholder for the post's unique identifier. We've also specified an alias (`as: 'post'`) for this route, which can be useful for generating URLs in views.

Request Parameters

When a client makes an HTTP request to your Rails application, it can include various parameters, which can be accessed by the controller actions. These parameters can come from different parts of the request, including the URL, query string, form data, or JSON payloads.

In the context of the routes we defined earlier, URL parameters are often used to pass information needed for the controller action. For instance, when a user visits /posts/1, Rails extracts the value 1 as the :id parameter.

You can access URL parameters in your controller action through the params hash. For example:

```ruby
class PostsController < ApplicationController
  def show
    post_id = params[:id]
    # Use post_id to find and display the corresponding post
  end
end
```

Here, we're extracting the :id parameter from the params hash to retrieve the post's identifier.

Query Parameters

Query parameters are often used in GET requests to provide additional information. For example, in a URL like /search?query=ruby, the query parameter is set to ruby. You can access query parameters similarly to URL parameters:

```ruby
class SearchController < ApplicationController
  def search
    search_query = params[:query]
    # Use search_query to perform a search operation
  end
end
```

In this example, we're extracting the query parameter from the params hash to perform a search operation based on the user's input.

Strong Parameters

In Rails, it's essential to be cautious about which parameters are allowed for mass assignment when creating or updating records. This is where Strong Parameters come into play. Strong Parameters are a security feature that helps protect your application from malicious input.

To use Strong Parameters, you typically define a private method in your controller to specify which parameters are permitted for mass assignment. For example:

```ruby
class PostsController < ApplicationController
  # ...

  private

  def post_params
```

```
    params.require(:post).permit(:title, :content)
  end
end
```

In this example, we're defining a post_params method that allows the :title and :content parameters to be mass-assigned when creating or updating a post. This helps prevent unwanted parameters from being used in mass assignments, enhancing the security of your application.

Conclusion

Handling HTTP requests is a fundamental aspect of building web applications in Ruby on Rails. By defining routes and using the params hash to access request parameters, you can route requests to the appropriate controller actions and interact with the data needed to provide responses. Strong Parameters further enhance the security of your application by controlling which parameters are permitted for mass assignment in record creation and updates. Understanding these concepts is crucial for effective Rails development.

6.3 Custom Routes and Route Constraints

In Ruby on Rails, the default routing mechanism is powerful and flexible. However, there are cases where you need more control over your application's routes. This is where custom routes and route constraints come into play. In this section, we'll explore how to define custom routes and use route constraints to tailor your application's routing behavior.

Custom Routes

Custom routes allow you to define your own routing rules that go beyond the standard RESTful routes generated by Rails. You can create routes for actions that don't follow the conventional CRUD operations or define routes that match specific URL patterns.

To define a custom route, you can use the match or get, post, put, or delete methods in your config/routes.rb file. Here's an example:

```ruby
# config/routes.rb
get '/about', to: 'pages#about'
```

In this example, we're creating a custom route that maps the URL /about to the about action of the PagesController. This allows you to create non-standard pages like an "About Us" page.

Route Constraints

Route constraints provide a way to conditionally match routes based on specific criteria, such as the host, subdomain, or request format. Constraints can be useful when you want to route requests to different controllers or actions based on specific conditions.

Let's say you want to route requests to different controllers based on the subdomain of the incoming request. You can define a route constraint like this:

```ruby
# config/routes.rb
constraints subdomain: 'api' do
  namespace :api do
    resources :posts
  end
end
```

In this example, requests with the subdomain 'api' will be routed to the `Api::PostsController`, allowing you to create a separate API namespace for your application.

Advanced Route Constraints

Route constraints can also be defined as custom Ruby classes that implement the `matches?` method. This method should return `true` if the constraint is met and `false` otherwise. This level of flexibility enables you to implement complex routing logic.

Here's an example of a custom route constraint that matches requests with specific query parameters:

```ruby
# app/constraints/query_parameter_constraint.rb
class QueryParameterConstraint
  def self.matches?(request)
    request.query_parameters.key?('special_param')
  end
end
```

You can then use this custom constraint in your routes:

```ruby
# config/routes.rb
get '/special_route', to: 'special#action', constraints: QueryParameterConstr
aint
```

In this example, the `QueryParameterConstraint` is used to check if the request includes a 'special_param' in its query parameters before routing to the 'special#action'.

Dynamic Segments

Custom routes can also include dynamic segments in the URL. Dynamic segments allow you to capture parts of the URL and pass them as parameters to your controller actions. For example:

```ruby
# config/routes.rb
get '/products/:id', to: 'products#show'
```

In this route, the `:id` segment is a dynamic segment that captures the product's identifier from the URL and passes it as a parameter to the `show` action of the `ProductsController`.

Conclusion

Custom routes and route constraints are powerful tools in Ruby on Rails that allow you to customize your application's routing behavior. They enable you to create non-standard routes, conditionally route requests based on criteria like subdomains or query parameters, and capture dynamic segments from the URL. By mastering these routing techniques, you can build flexible and sophisticated web applications tailored to your specific requirements.

6.4 Working with Filters and Middleware

In Ruby on Rails, filters and middleware play a crucial role in intercepting and processing incoming HTTP requests before they reach the controller actions. Filters allow you to add logic that runs before, after, or around controller actions, while middleware operates at a lower level and can be applied globally to the entire application. In this section, we'll explore filters and middleware and how they can enhance your application.

Filters in Rails

Filters are methods that are executed before, after, or around controller actions. They are useful for tasks such as authentication, authorization, logging, and more. Filters can be applied to specific controller actions or to all actions within a controller.

Before Filters

Before filters are executed before a controller action is invoked. They are commonly used for tasks like authentication and authorization. To define a before filter, you can use the before_action method in your controller:

```ruby
class ApplicationController < ActionController::Base
  before_action :authenticate_user

  private

  def authenticate_user
    # Logic to check if the user is authenticated
  end
end
```

In this example, the authenticate_user method is a before filter that will be executed before any action in controllers that inherit from ApplicationController. You can define and use multiple before filters in your controllers.

After filters are executed after a controller action has completed. They are less commonly used but can be handy for tasks like logging or cleanup. You can define an after filter using the after_action method:

```
class ApplicationController < ActionController::Base
  after_action :log_action

  private

  def log_action
    # Logic to log the completed action
  end
end
```

Here, the log_action method is an after filter that runs after the controller action has finished.

Around Filters

Around filters allow you to wrap a controller action with custom code that runs both before and after the action. This can be useful for tasks that require setup and cleanup. You can define an around filter using the around_action method:

```
class ApplicationController < ActionController::Base
  around_action :transactional_action

  private

  def transactional_action
    ActiveRecord::Base.transaction do
      yield
    end
  end
end
```

In this example, the transactional_action method is an around filter that wraps the controller action in a database transaction.

Middleware in Rails

Middleware is a lower-level concept than filters and operates at the Rack level in a Rails application. Middleware components are designed to process requests and responses globally, affecting the entire application. They can perform tasks like authentication, logging, and response manipulation.

Rails comes with several built-in middleware components, and you can also create custom middleware for your application.

To use middleware in your Rails application, you can configure them in the `config/application.rb` file:

```
config.middleware.use MyCustomMiddleware
```

This configuration will insert `MyCustomMiddleware` into the middleware stack, affecting all incoming requests.

Conclusion

Filters and middleware are essential components of Ruby on Rails that enable you to add pre- and post-processing logic to your application. Filters are controller-specific and allow you to control the flow of actions within a controller, while middleware operates at a lower level and affects the entire application. Understanding how to use filters and middleware effectively can help you implement various functionalities such as authentication, logging, and response manipulation in your Rails applications.

6.5 Implementing Authentication with Devise

Authentication is a crucial aspect of web applications, ensuring that users are who they claim to be. Ruby on Rails provides numerous tools and gems to simplify the process of implementing authentication. One of the most popular and feature-rich authentication solutions for Rails is Devise. In this section, we'll explore how to implement authentication using Devise in your Rails application.

What is Devise?

Devise is a flexible authentication solution for Rails that offers a wide range of features out of the box. It provides user registration, login, password reset, session management, and more. Devise is highly customizable, allowing you to tailor authentication to your application's specific needs.

Adding Devise to Your Rails Application

To use Devise in your Rails application, you need to add it to your Gemfile and run bundle install:

```
# Gemfile
gem 'devise'
```

After adding Devise to your Gemfile, run:

```
bundle install
```

Next, you need to run the Devise generator to set up the required files and configurations:

```
rails generate devise:install
```

This command will create a `config/initializers/devise.rb` file with configuration options.

Creating a User Model

To implement authentication, you'll typically need a User model. You can generate it using Devise:

```
rails generate devise User
```

This command will generate a User model with the necessary attributes for authentication, such as email and password. It will also create a migration to add the required columns to your database.

Running Migrations

After generating the User model, run the database migration to create the User table:

```
rails db:migrate
```

Configuring Routes

Devise automatically generates routes for user registration, login, and other authentication-related actions. You can customize these routes in your `config/routes.rb` file. For example:

```ruby
# config/routes.rb
devise_for :users, controllers: {
  sessions: 'users/sessions',
  registrations: 'users/registrations'
}
```

This code customizes the routes for user sessions (login) and registrations (sign-up) by specifying custom controllers.

Customizing Views

Devise provides default views for authentication-related actions, but you can customize them to match your application's design. You can generate the views using the Devise generator:

```
rails generate devise:views
```

This will create a `views/devise` folder in your application with the authentication-related view templates.

Using Devise Helpers

Devise offers a set of helpers that you can use in your controllers and views to manage authentication. For example, you can use `current_user` to access the currently signed-in user in your controllers or views.

```ruby
# In a controller
def some_action
  if user_signed_in?
    # Perform actions for authenticated users
  else
    # Redirect or display a message for unauthenticated users
  end
end
```

Conclusion

Implementing authentication with Devise in your Ruby on Rails application is a straightforward and powerful way to add user registration, login, and session management features. By following the steps outlined in this section, you can quickly integrate Devise into your application and secure your users' access to your system. Remember that Devise is highly customizable, allowing you to adapt authentication to your specific requirements while benefiting from its robust feature set.

Chapter 7: Testing Your Rails Application

7.1 The Importance of Testing in Rails

Testing is a fundamental practice in software development, and Ruby on Rails provides a robust testing framework to help you ensure the correctness and reliability of your applications. In this section, we'll explore the importance of testing in Rails development and introduce you to the different types of tests commonly used in Rails projects.

Why Testing Matters

Testing plays a crucial role in the software development lifecycle for several reasons:

1. Detecting Bugs and Errors

Testing helps identify and catch bugs, errors, and unexpected behavior in your application. By writing tests, you can systematically verify that different parts of your code work as intended.

2. Maintaining Code Quality

Tests serve as a form of documentation for your codebase. They provide a clear understanding of how various components of your application should behave, making it easier for you and your team to maintain code quality over time.

3. Supporting Refactoring

Refactoring, the process of improving code without changing its external behavior, is a common practice in Rails development. Tests act as a safety net, ensuring that your code remains correct after refactoring.

4. Enhancing Collaboration

Tests enable better collaboration among team members. When multiple developers work on a project, having a comprehensive test suite ensures that changes made by one developer don't break existing functionality.

Types of Tests in Rails

Rails encourages a testing philosophy that encompasses several types of tests, each serving a specific purpose:

1. Unit Tests

Unit tests, also known as model tests, focus on individual components of your application, such as models and their methods. These tests verify that specific methods and behaviors of your code work correctly in isolation.

2. Functional Tests

Functional tests, often referred to as controller tests, check the behavior of controller actions in response to HTTP requests. They ensure that the controllers handle requests and produce the expected responses.

3. Integration Tests

Integration tests examine how different parts of your application work together. They test the interactions between controllers, models, and views, ensuring that the various components collaborate seamlessly.

4. System Tests

System tests, also known as end-to-end tests, simulate the behavior of a user interacting with your application. These tests check the entire application stack, including the user interface and database interactions, to ensure that the application functions correctly from a user's perspective.

5. Acceptance Tests

Acceptance tests are high-level tests that focus on user stories and the application's overall functionality. They ensure that the application meets the requirements and expectations of users and stakeholders.

Writing Tests in Rails

Rails provides a testing framework based on the concept of Test-Driven Development (TDD). In TDD, you write tests before implementing the actual code. Here's a basic process for writing tests in Rails:

1. Define the behavior: Clearly specify what a particular piece of code is supposed to do.
2. Write a test: Create a test that checks whether the defined behavior is met.
3. Run the test: Execute the test to see if it fails, as it should since you haven't implemented the code yet.
4. Write code: Implement the code necessary to make the test pass.
5. Run the test again: Execute the test to verify that your code now passes it.
6. Refactor (if needed): Once the test passes, you can refactor your code if necessary while maintaining test coverage.

By following this process, you can iteratively develop your application, ensuring that it remains reliable and behaves as expected throughout its lifecycle.

Conclusion

Testing is a crucial practice in Ruby on Rails development. It helps maintain code quality, detect and prevent bugs, support refactoring, and enhance collaboration among team members. Understanding the different types of tests available in Rails and following a test-driven development approach can significantly improve the reliability and maintainability of your Rails applications. In the following sections, we will delve deeper into each type of test and explore the tools and best practices for effective testing in Rails.

7.2 Writing Unit Tests with RSpec

RSpec is a popular testing framework for Ruby that is commonly used in the Ruby on Rails ecosystem. In this section, we'll explore how to write unit tests for your Rails application using RSpec. Unit tests focus on testing individual components of your application, such as models and their methods.

Why RSpec?

RSpec provides a highly readable and expressive syntax for writing tests, making it a favorite choice among Ruby and Rails developers. It follows the Behavior-Driven Development (BDD) approach, which encourages writing tests in a human-readable language that closely resembles the way developers discuss and think about software behavior.

Setting Up RSpec

To use RSpec in your Rails application, you'll need to add it to your Gemfile:

```ruby
# Gemfile
group :development, :test do
  gem 'rspec-rails', '~> 5.0'
end
```

After adding RSpec to your Gemfile, run the following commands:

```
bundle install
rails generate rspec:install
```

This will generate the necessary configuration files for RSpec and set up your Rails application for testing with RSpec.

Writing Your First Unit Test

Let's start by writing a unit test for a model in your Rails application. Suppose you have a User model with a full_name method that concatenates the first name and last name. Here's how you can write a unit test for this method using RSpec:

```ruby
# spec/models/user_spec.rb

require 'rails_helper'

RSpec.describe User, type: :model do
  it 'concatenates first name and last name to create full name' do
```

```
    user = User.new(first_name: 'John', last_name: 'Doe')
    expect(user.full_name).to eq('John Doe')
  end
end
```

In this example, we use the `RSpec.describe` method to define a test suite for the `User` model. Inside the test suite, we use the `it` method to specify an individual test case. We create a `User` instance, call the `full_name` method, and use `expect` to make an assertion that the result matches our expectation.

Running RSpec Tests

To run your RSpec tests, you can use the following command:

```
rspec
```

RSpec will discover and execute all the tests in your Rails application. If you want to run a specific test file or directory, you can provide the file or directory path as an argument to the `rspec` command.

Additional RSpec Matchers

RSpec provides a wide range of matchers to make your tests more expressive and readable. For example, you can use `expect(object).to be_valid` to check if an object is valid according to its model validations, or `expect(collection).to include(item)` to check if a collection includes a specific item.

Conclusion

Writing unit tests with RSpec in your Ruby on Rails application is a valuable practice to ensure the correctness of your model methods. RSpec's expressive syntax and extensive set of matchers make it a powerful tool for writing and maintaining tests. By following the principles of Behavior-Driven Development (BDD) and writing clear and readable tests, you can improve the reliability and maintainability of your Rails models. In the upcoming sections, we'll explore other types of tests in Rails and how to use them effectively.

7.3 Integration Testing with Capybara

Integration testing is an essential part of ensuring that your Ruby on Rails application functions correctly from the user's perspective. In this section, we'll delve into integration testing using Capybara, a popular tool for simulating user interactions with your application.

What is Capybara?

Capybara is a Ruby library that allows you to write expressive and readable integration tests for web applications. It provides a high-level API for interacting with web pages and elements, making it an excellent choice for testing the full stack of your Rails application.

Setting Up Capybara

To use Capybara in your Rails project, you need to include it in your Gemfile:

```ruby
# Gemfile
group :test do
  gem 'capybara', '~> 3.0'
end
```

After adding Capybara to your Gemfile, run `bundle install` to install the gem.

Writing Your First Capybara Test

Let's start by writing a simple integration test using Capybara. Suppose you want to test the functionality of a user registration form. Here's an example test:

```ruby
# spec/features/user_registration_spec.rb

require 'rails_helper'

RSpec.feature 'User Registration', type: :feature do
  scenario 'User can register with valid information' do
    visit new_user_registration_path

    fill_in 'Email', with: 'user@example.com'
    fill_in 'Password', with: 'password'
    fill_in 'Password confirmation', with: 'password'

    click_button 'Sign up'

    expect(page).to have_text('Welcome! You have signed up successfully.')
  end
end
```

In this example, we use the `RSpec.feature` method to define a feature test. Inside the test, we use Capybara's methods like `visit`, `fill_in`, and `click_button` to interact with the user registration form and simulate the user's actions. Finally, we use `expect` to make an assertion about the content displayed on the page.

Running Capybara Tests

To run your Capybara tests, you can use the same `rspec` command as for other RSpec tests:

```
rspec
```

Capybara will execute your feature tests, launch a web browser (typically a headless browser like Selenium or ChromeDriver), and simulate user interactions as defined in your tests.

Capybara Matchers

Capybara provides a set of matchers that you can use in your tests to make assertions about the state of the page. For example, you can use `expect(page).to have_text('Welcome!')` to check if the page contains a specific text.

Choosing a Driver

Capybara supports multiple drivers for interacting with web applications, including RackTest (a lightweight driver), Selenium (for browser automation), and more. You can configure the driver you want to use in your test environment's configuration file (e.g., `spec/rails_helper.rb`).

Conclusion

Integration testing with Capybara is a valuable practice to ensure that your Rails application functions correctly from the user's perspective. By simulating user interactions with your application, you can catch issues that may not be apparent in unit tests. Capybara's expressive API and extensive set of matchers make it a powerful tool for writing and maintaining integration tests in your Rails project. In the upcoming sections, we'll explore other testing techniques and best practices in Rails development.

7.4 Continuous Integration with Travis CI

Continuous Integration (CI) is a crucial practice in modern software development that involves automatically building, testing, and deploying code changes to ensure the project's stability and quality. In this section, we'll explore how to set up Continuous Integration for your Ruby on Rails project using Travis CI.

What is Travis CI?

Travis CI is a cloud-based CI/CD (Continuous Integration/Continuous Deployment) service that integrates seamlessly with GitHub and other version control systems. It automates the process of building and testing your application whenever changes are pushed to the repository.

Setting Up Travis CI for Your Rails Project

To set up Travis CI for your Rails project, follow these steps:

1. **Create a Travis CI Account**: If you don't have a Travis CI account, sign up for one at https://travis-ci.com. You can use your GitHub account to sign in.

2. **Enable Your Repository**: In your Travis CI dashboard, enable the repository that contains your Rails project. This will trigger Travis CI builds whenever you push changes to the repository.

3. **Create a `.travis.yml` File**: In your project's root directory, create a `.travis.yml` file. This file defines the build configuration for Travis CI. Here's a basic example for a Ruby on Rails project:

```
language: ruby
rvm:
  - 2.7.3
services:
  - postgresql
before_script:
  - bundle install
  - bundle exec rails db:create db:migrate
script:
  - bundle exec rspec
```

This configuration specifies the Ruby version, sets up a PostgreSQL database, runs database migrations, and then runs your RSpec tests.

4. **Commit and Push**: Commit the `.travis.yml` file to your repository and push the changes to GitHub. This will trigger the first Travis CI build.

5. **Monitor Builds**: You can monitor the status of your builds in the Travis CI dashboard or directly in your GitHub repository. Travis CI will automatically build your project when you push changes, and you can see the results of each build, including whether tests passed or failed.

Benefits of Travis CI

Travis CI offers several benefits for your Rails project:

- **Automated Testing**: Travis CI automatically runs your tests whenever changes are pushed, ensuring that your application remains in a working state.

- **Integration with GitHub**: Travis CI seamlessly integrates with GitHub, making it easy to trigger builds and view build statuses directly in your repository.

- **Parallel Testing**: Travis CI can distribute your tests across multiple workers, allowing for faster test execution, especially in larger projects.

- **Deployment**: You can configure Travis CI to automatically deploy your Rails application to your hosting environment after successful builds, enabling Continuous Deployment (CD).

- **Open Source**: Travis CI offers free plans for open-source projects, making it an excellent choice for community-driven Rails projects.

Conclusion

Continuous Integration with Travis CI is a valuable practice for ensuring the quality and stability of your Ruby on Rails project. By automating the build and testing process, you can catch issues early, collaborate effectively with your team, and deliver reliable software to your users. In the next section, we'll explore debugging and troubleshooting techniques in Rails development.

7.5 Debugging and Troubleshooting Techniques

Debugging is an essential skill for any developer, and it becomes particularly crucial when working with Ruby on Rails applications. In this section, we'll explore debugging and troubleshooting techniques to help you identify and resolve issues in your Rails projects efficiently.

1. Debugging Tools

Pry Debugger

Pry is a powerful runtime developer console for Ruby. You can insert `binding.pry` statements into your code to pause execution and start an interactive console session right in the context of your application. This allows you to inspect variables, run code, and diagnose issues effectively.

```
# Example usage of Pry in a Rails controller action
def some_action
  # ...
  binding.pry
  # ...
end
```

Byebug

Byebug is another popular debugger for Ruby. It provides similar functionality to Pry and is often a matter of personal preference among developers.

```
# Example usage of Byebug in a Rails controller action
def some_action
  # ...
  byebug
  # ...
end
```

2. Logging

Rails comes with a built-in logging system that you can use to track the flow of your application and log information for debugging purposes. You can add custom log entries using the `Rails.logger` object.

```
# Logging a custom message
Rails.logger.debug('This is a debug message')
Rails.logger.info('This is an info message')
Rails.logger.warn('This is a warning message')
```

```
Rails.logger.error('This is an error message')
Rails.logger.fatal('This is a fatal message')
```

You can find the logs in the `log/` directory of your Rails application, with different log levels separated into their respective files.

3. Error Pages and Exception Handling

Rails provides a robust exception handling mechanism that allows you to rescue and handle exceptions gracefully. You can customize error pages and actions to provide meaningful feedback to users and log detailed information about errors.

```
# Handling an exception and rendering a custom error page
class ApplicationController < ActionController::Base
  rescue_from StandardError, with: :render_error

  private

  def render_error(exception)
    Rails.logger.error(exception.message)
    render 'errors/500', status: :internal_server_error
  end
end
```

4. Database Queries

When dealing with database-related issues, you can use the Rails console to execute queries and inspect data interactively. This can help you identify data-related problems and test SQL queries.

```
# Access the Rails console
rails console
```

```
# Example: Fetching records from a model
User.where(email: 'example@example.com')
```

5. Third-Party Tools

Consider using third-party monitoring and error tracking tools like New Relic, Sentry, or Rollbar to gain insights into your application's performance and receive real-time alerts when errors occur.

6. Testing and Test-Driven Development (TDD)

Adopting Test-Driven Development (TDD) practices by writing tests before implementing features can help prevent bugs and make troubleshooting easier. Test suites provide a safety net for your code and can pinpoint issues when they arise.

7. Collaborate and Seek Help

Don't hesitate to seek help from your team or the Rails community when you're stuck on a problem. Websites like Stack Overflow and Rails-specific forums can be valuable resources for troubleshooting and resolving issues.

Conclusion

Debugging and troubleshooting are essential skills for Rails developers. Whether you're diagnosing runtime errors, investigating database issues, or fine-tuning your application's performance, these techniques will help you identify and resolve problems effectively. Remember that debugging is not just about fixing errors but also about understanding your code better and improving its overall quality.

Chapter 8: Enhancing Your Application with JavaScript and AJAX

8.1 Introduction to JavaScript in Rails

JavaScript is a crucial component of modern web development, and it plays a significant role in enhancing the interactivity and responsiveness of your Ruby on Rails applications. In this section, we'll introduce you to JavaScript in the context of Rails development and explore how you can use it to create dynamic user interfaces and make asynchronous requests using AJAX (Asynchronous JavaScript and XML).

Why JavaScript in Rails?

Rails primarily relies on server-side rendering to generate HTML pages. However, for more interactive and dynamic features, JavaScript is essential. Here are some reasons to use JavaScript in your Rails applications:

1. **User Experience**: JavaScript allows you to create dynamic, interactive user interfaces that respond to user actions in real-time, providing a more engaging user experience.

2. **AJAX**: Asynchronous JavaScript and XML (AJAX) enables you to fetch and update data from the server without requiring a full page reload. This leads to faster and smoother interactions.

3. **Front-End Frameworks**: Many front-end frameworks like React, Vue.js, and Angular integrate seamlessly with Rails to build complex single-page applications (SPAs).

Including JavaScript in Rails

Rails makes it easy to include JavaScript in your application. By default, Rails uses the Asset Pipeline to manage and serve JavaScript files. You can find JavaScript files in the `app/assets/javascripts` directory.

To include a JavaScript file in a view or layout, use the `javascript_include_tag` helper method. For example:

```
<%= javascript_include_tag 'application' %>
```

This includes the `application.js` file, which typically contains JavaScript that's used across your entire application.

Unobtrusive JavaScript

Rails promotes the use of unobtrusive JavaScript, which separates JavaScript behavior from HTML markup. Instead of adding JavaScript directly to HTML elements, you can use data attributes to define behavior and then attach event listeners in your JavaScript files.

For example, in your HTML:

```html
<button data-behavior="clickable">Click Me</button>
```

In your JavaScript file:

```javascript
document.addEventListener('DOMContentLoaded', function() {
  const clickableButton = document.querySelector('[data-behavior="clickable"]');

  clickableButton.addEventListener('click', function() {
    alert('Button Clicked!');
  });
});
```

This approach keeps your HTML clean and maintainable while allowing you to enhance it with JavaScript interactions.

AJAX in Rails

Rails provides built-in support for making AJAX requests. You can use the `remote: true` option in form submissions or links to trigger AJAX requests.

```erb
<%= form_for @post, remote: true do |f| %>
  <!-- Form fields here -->
  <%= f.submit 'Create Post' %>
<% end %>
```

In your controller, you can respond to AJAX requests with JavaScript views (`.js.erb` files) that update the page without a full reload.

```ruby
# posts_controller.rb
def create
  @post = Post.new(post_params)

  if @post.save
    respond_to do |format|
      format.html { redirect_to @post }
      format.js   # Renders create.js.erb
    end
  else
    # Handle errors
  end
end
```

In `create.js.erb`, you can write JavaScript code to update the page dynamically.

```javascript
// create.js.erb
document.getElementById('posts-container').innerHTML += '<%= j render @post %>';
```

This example appends the newly created post to the page without a refresh.

Conclusion

JavaScript is a vital tool for enhancing the interactivity and responsiveness of your Ruby on Rails applications. Whether you're using it for small interactions or building complex single-page applications, Rails provides the tools and conventions to work with JavaScript effectively and maintainably. In the next sections, we'll delve deeper into AJAX, real-time features with WebSockets, and integrating JavaScript libraries and front-end frameworks with Rails.

8.2 Making AJAX Requests

Making AJAX (Asynchronous JavaScript and XML) requests is a fundamental part of building dynamic and responsive web applications with Ruby on Rails. AJAX allows you to fetch and send data to the server without the need to reload the entire page, resulting in a smoother user experience. In this section, we'll explore how to make AJAX requests in Rails.

1. Using remote: true

In Rails, you can easily make AJAX requests by leveraging the `remote: true` option in your forms and links. When you set `remote: true`, Rails automatically generates the necessary JavaScript code to send the form or link request asynchronously.

For example, you can create an AJAX form like this:

```erb
<%= form_for @post, remote: true do |f| %>
  <!-- Form fields here -->
  <%= f.submit 'Create Post' %>
<% end %>
```

When the form is submitted, Rails sends an AJAX request to the server, and you can handle it like any other form submission in your controller. To respond with JavaScript, you can use a JavaScript view (`.js.erb`).

2. Handling AJAX Requests in the Controller

In your controller, you can detect AJAX requests using the `request.xhr?` method. For example:

```ruby
def create
  @post = Post.new(post_params)

  respond_to do |format|
    if @post.save
      format.html { redirect_to @post }
      format.js    # Renders create.js.erb for AJAX requests
    else
      # Handle errors
    end
```

```
    end
end
```

Here, when the `create` action is called via an AJAX request, it responds with JavaScript (`format.js`), allowing you to update the page dynamically in the associated `.js.erb` view.

3. Updating the Page with JavaScript

In your JavaScript views (`.js.erb`), you can write JavaScript code to update the page based on the server's response. For example, after creating a new post, you can append it to a list of posts without reloading the entire page:

```
// create.js.erb
$('#posts-container').append('<%= j render @post %>');
```

This JavaScript code uses jQuery to append the newly created post's HTML representation to an element with the `posts-container` ID.

4. Using Data Attributes

To pass data between the server and JavaScript, you can use data attributes. In your views, you can set data attributes on HTML elements:

```
<div id="user" data-user-id="<%= @user.id %>" data-user-name="<%= @user.name %>">
  <!-- User content here -->
</div>
```

Then, in your JavaScript, you can access these data attributes:

```
const userDiv = document.getElementById('user');
const userId = userDiv.getAttribute('data-user-id');
const userName = userDiv.getAttribute('data-user-name');
```

5. AJAX and Error Handling

When making AJAX requests, it's crucial to handle errors gracefully. You can use the `error` callback in your JavaScript to manage error responses from the server and provide appropriate feedback to the user.

```
$.ajax({
  url: '/some_endpoint',
  method: 'GET',
  success: function(response) {
    // Handle successful response
  },
  error: function(xhr, status, error) {
    // Handle error response
    console.error('Error:', error);
  }
});
```

This example uses jQuery's `$.ajax` method to make a GET request to `/some_endpoint` and handles both successful and error responses.

AJAX requests are a powerful tool for enhancing the interactivity of your Ruby on Rails applications. By leveraging Rails' built-in support for AJAX and creating JavaScript views, you can create dynamic and responsive user interfaces that provide a better user experience. In the next sections, we'll explore more advanced topics, including real-time features with WebSockets and integrating JavaScript libraries and frameworks with Rails.

8.3 Implementing Real-Time Features with WebSockets

WebSockets provide a powerful mechanism for enabling real-time features in your Ruby on Rails applications. Unlike traditional HTTP requests, which are stateless and typically require polling for updates, WebSockets offer a full-duplex communication channel between the client and the server. In this section, we'll explore how to implement real-time features using WebSockets in Rails.

1. The Need for Real-Time Features

Real-time features are essential for applications that require live updates, such as chat applications, notifications, and collaborative tools. WebSockets allow you to establish a persistent connection between the client and server, enabling instant data transfer in both directions.

2. Action Cable in Rails

Action Cable is a built-in Rails framework for handling WebSocket connections. It seamlessly integrates WebSockets into your Rails application, making it relatively straightforward to implement real-time features.

To use Action Cable, you need to set up a WebSocket server alongside your Rails application. The most common choice is to use Redis as the message broker for Action Cable.

3. Setting Up Action Cable

To get started with Action Cable, you need to configure it in your Rails application:

1. Add the gem `'redis'` to your Gemfile and run `bundle install` to install the Redis gem.

2. Configure Redis in your `config/cable.yml` file:

```
development:
  adapter: redis
  url: redis://localhost:6379/1
```

3. Create a channel to define the WebSocket behavior. You can use the `rails generate` channel command to generate a channel file.

4. Define the WebSocket behavior in the generated channel file. For example, you can create a chat channel to handle real-time chat messages.

```ruby
# app/channels/chat_channel.rb
class ChatChannel < ApplicationCable::Channel
  def subscribed
    stream_from 'chat_channel'
  end

  def receive(data)
    # Handle received data (e.g., broadcast the message)
    ActionCable.server.broadcast('chat_channel', message: data['message'])
  end

  def unsubscribed
    # Cleanup when the WebSocket connection is closed
  end
end
```

4. JavaScript Integration

On the client-side, you'll need to write JavaScript to establish a WebSocket connection and interact with the server. You can use Action Cable's JavaScript library to simplify this process.

Here's an example of JavaScript code that subscribes to the ChatChannel and sends and receives messages:

```javascript
// app/assets/javascripts/cable.js
import consumer from "./consumer"

consumer.subscriptions.create("ChatChannel", {
  connected() {
    // Called when the WebSocket connection is established
  },

  disconnected() {
    // Called when the WebSocket connection is closed
  },

  received(data) {
    // Called when data is received from the WebSocket
    console.log(data.message);
  },

  speak(message) {
    // Send data to the server
```

```
      this.perform('speak', { message: message });
  }
});
```

5. Broadcasting Messages

In your Rails controllers or background jobs, you can use Action Cable to broadcast
messages to subscribed WebSocket channels. For example, in a chat application, when a
new message is created, you can broadcast it to all connected clients.

```ruby
# app/controllers/messages_controller.rb
def create
  @message = Message.new(message_params)

  if @message.save
    ActionCable.server.broadcast('chat_channel', message: @message.content)
    # Additional handling here
  else
    # Handle errors
  end
end
```

6. Handling Multiple Channels

You can create and handle multiple WebSocket channels for different real-time features in
your application. Each channel should have its logic and can be subscribed to
independently on the client-side.

Conclusion

Implementing real-time features with WebSockets using Action Cable in Ruby on Rails
opens up new possibilities for creating dynamic and interactive applications. Whether
you're building a chat application, a live notification system, or collaborative tools,
WebSockets provide a robust foundation for delivering instant updates to your users. In
the following sections, we'll explore further enhancements to your Rails application,
including the use of JavaScript libraries and front-end frameworks.

8.4 Using JavaScript Libraries (e.g., jQuery)

JavaScript libraries like jQuery can significantly simplify the process of enhancing your
Ruby on Rails application's interactivity and functionality. In this section, we'll explore how
to integrate jQuery into your Rails project and leverage its features for tasks such as DOM
manipulation, AJAX requests, and event handling.

1. Integrating jQuery

To use jQuery in your Rails application, follow these steps:

1. Add the jQuery gem to your Gemfile and run `bundle install`:

    ```
    gem 'jquery-rails'
    ```

2. Include jQuery in your application's JavaScript manifest file (`application.js`):

    ```
    //= require jquery
    //= require jquery_ujs
    ```

    The `jquery_ujs` file includes features like AJAX handling for Rails applications.

3. Ensure that jQuery is loaded before other JavaScript files that depend on it.

2. Basic DOM Manipulation

jQuery simplifies DOM manipulation tasks, making it easier to select and manipulate elements on your web pages. For example, to hide an element with a specific ID:

```
$(document).ready(function() {
  $('#my-element').hide();
});
```

The `$(document).ready` function ensures that your code runs after the document has finished loading.

3. Event Handling

jQuery makes it straightforward to handle events such as clicks, form submissions, and keypresses. Here's an example of binding a click event to a button element:

```
$(document).ready(function() {
  $('#my-button').click(function() {
    // Code to execute when the button is clicked
  });
});
```

4. AJAX Requests with jQuery

You can use jQuery to make AJAX requests in your Rails application. Here's an example of making a GET request:

```
$(document).ready(function() {
  $('#load-data-button').click(function() {
    $.ajax({
      url: '/data_endpoint',
      method: 'GET',
      success: function(response) {
        // Handle the successful response
      },
      error: function(xhr, status, error) {
        // Handle the error response
      }
```

```
    });
  });
});
```

5. Working with Forms

jQuery simplifies form handling, allowing you to capture form submissions, validate input, and submit data via AJAX. For instance, you can prevent the default form submission and handle it asynchronously:

```
$(document).ready(function() {
  $('#my-form').submit(function(event) {
    event.preventDefault(); // Prevent the default form submission

    // Perform form validation here

    // Send data via AJAX
    $.ajax({
      url: '/submit_endpoint',
      method: 'POST',
      data: $(this).serialize(), // Serialize form data
      success: function(response) {
        // Handle the successful response
      },
      error: function(xhr, status, error) {
        // Handle the error response
      }
    });
  });
});
```

6. jQuery Plugins and Enhancements

jQuery offers a vast ecosystem of plugins that can extend its functionality further. You can find plugins for tasks like creating sliders, implementing date pickers, and managing complex UI components. These plugins can save you development time and effort when building rich web applications.

Conclusion

Integrating jQuery into your Ruby on Rails application empowers you to create more interactive and dynamic user interfaces. Whether you need to manipulate the DOM, handle user events, make AJAX requests, or use jQuery plugins, this library provides a versatile toolset for enhancing your web application's functionality. In the next section, we'll delve into integrating front-end frameworks like React or Vue.js with Rails for even more advanced features and interactivity.

8.5 Front-End Frameworks and Integration with Rails

Front-end frameworks like React, Vue.js, and Angular provide powerful tools for building modern, interactive web applications. In this section, we'll explore how to integrate these front-end frameworks with your Ruby on Rails backend, enabling you to create feature-rich and responsive web applications.

1. Choosing a Front-End Framework

Before integrating a front-end framework, you should choose the one that best suits your project's requirements. Some popular options include:

- **React**: Developed by Facebook, React is known for building dynamic user interfaces and is often used in single-page applications (SPAs).
- **Vue.js**: Vue is a progressive framework that's easy to adopt incrementally. It's known for its simplicity and flexibility.
- **Angular**: Developed by Google, Angular is a comprehensive framework that provides a full set of tools for building complex web applications.

2. Setting Up a Rails API

To integrate a front-end framework, you'll typically create a Rails API to serve as the backend. This API will handle data storage, authentication, and other server-side tasks while allowing the front-end framework to manage the user interface and application logic.

1. Start by generating a new Rails application with the `--api` flag to create a minimal Rails API:

    ```
    rails new my_api --api
    ```

2. Configure your API routes and controllers to expose the necessary endpoints for your front-end framework.

3. Implement authentication and authorization mechanisms if required for your application.

3. Front-End Integration

React Integration

If you're integrating React, you can use the `react-rails` gem to simplify the process. Install the gem and run the generator:

```
gem install react-rails
rails generate react:install
```

This will set up the necessary files and configurations for integrating React components into your Rails views.

To integrate Vue.js, you can use the `vuejs` gem, which provides a Vue.js Rails generator:

```
gem install vuejs
rails generate vuejs:install
```

This generator will set up Vue.js in your Rails application and configure the necessary files and settings.

4. Building Front-End Components

Once your front-end framework is integrated, you can start building components for your user interface. These components can manage the display and interaction of specific parts of your application.

For example, if you're using React, you can create a component like this:

```javascript
// app/javascript/components/ExampleComponent.js
import React from 'react';

class ExampleComponent extends React.Component {
  render() {
    return (
      <div>
        <h1>Hello, React!</h1>
      </div>
    );
  }
}

export default ExampleComponent;
```

5. Making API Requests

Front-end frameworks often need to communicate with the Rails API to fetch data, submit forms, or perform other actions. You can use libraries like `axios` for making API requests in React or `axios-rails` for integrating it with Rails.

6. Authentication and Authorization

Ensure that your front-end framework handles user authentication and authorization. You can use tokens or cookies to authenticate users and protect sensitive routes and actions.

Conclusion

Integrating front-end frameworks with Ruby on Rails enables you to build modern, interactive web applications that offer a seamless user experience. By leveraging the strengths of both the backend and front-end technologies, you can create feature-rich and responsive applications that meet the demands of today's web development landscape. In the next chapters, we'll dive deeper into specific topics such as RESTful API development, deployment, performance optimization, and security.

Chapter 9: RESTful API Development with Rails

In this chapter, we'll delve into the world of building RESTful APIs (Application Programming Interfaces) with Ruby on Rails. RESTful APIs are a crucial part of modern web development, allowing your application to communicate with other services, mobile apps, or external clients. We'll explore the principles of REST and how Rails simplifies the process of creating APIs.

9.1 Understanding RESTful Principles

REST (Representational State Transfer) is an architectural style for designing networked applications. It provides a set of constraints and principles that, when followed, lead to scalable, maintainable, and predictable APIs. Here are some key principles of REST:

1. Resource-Based

In REST, everything is a resource, which is identified by a URL (Uniform Resource Locator). Resources can represent data entities such as users, products, or articles. For example, a user resource might be represented by the URL /users.

2. CRUD Operations

RESTful APIs map CRUD (Create, Read, Update, Delete) operations to standard HTTP methods:

- GET: Used for retrieving resource representations.
- POST: Used for creating new resources.
- PUT or PATCH: Used for updating existing resources.
- DELETE: Used for deleting resources.

3. Stateless

Each request to a RESTful API must contain all the information required to understand and process the request. The server should not store any client state. This makes APIs scalable and easy to maintain.

4. Uniform Interface

RESTful APIs should have a consistent and uniform interface. This includes using standard HTTP methods, status codes, and URLs. For example, using the HTTP status code 200 OK for successful responses and 404 Not Found for resource not found.

5. Representation

Resources can have multiple representations, such as JSON, XML, or HTML. Clients can request the representation that best suits their needs using the Accept header.

6. HATEOAS (Hypermedia as the Engine of Application State)

HATEOAS is a principle that suggests including hyperlinks in the API response to guide clients on what actions they can take next. This makes the API more self-descriptive and reduces the need for clients to have prior knowledge of the API structure.

Building RESTful APIs in Rails

Ruby on Rails provides a robust framework for building RESTful APIs that adhere to these principles. Rails' conventions make it easy to define routes, controllers, and serializers for your API endpoints. In the next sections, we'll dive deeper into building API endpoints, securing them with authentication, versioning, and documenting them using tools like Swagger.

9.2 Building API Endpoints

In this section, we'll focus on building API endpoints using Ruby on Rails. API endpoints are URLs that clients can use to interact with your application programmatically. We'll cover the basics of defining and structuring API routes, creating controllers to handle requests, and returning JSON responses.

Defining API Routes

In Rails, you can define API routes in the `config/routes.rb` file. To create a new route for a resource, you can use the `resources` method. For example, to define routes for a `User` resource, you can do the following:

```ruby
# config/routes.rb
Rails.application.routes.draw do
  namespace :api, defaults: { format: :json } do
    resources :users
  end
end
```

In this example, we've defined a `users` resource within the `api` namespace. This sets up routes for creating, reading, updating, and deleting users.

Creating API Controllers

API controllers handle incoming requests and prepare JSON responses. You can generate a controller for your API resource using the Rails generator:

```
rails generate controller api/users
```

This generates a controller file named `api/users_controller.rb` where you can define actions to handle various API requests:

```ruby
# app/controllers/api/users_controller.rb
class Api::UsersController < ApplicationController
  before_action :set_user, only: [:show, :update, :destroy]

  # GET /api/users
  def index
    @users = User.all
    render json: @users
  end

  # GET /api/users/1
  def show
    render json: @user
  end

  # POST /api/users
  def create
    @user = User.new(user_params)

    if @user.save
      render json: @user, status: :created
    else
      render json: @user.errors, status: :unprocessable_entity
    end
  end

  # PATCH/PUT /api/users/1
  def update
    if @user.update(user_params)
      render json: @user
    else
      render json: @user.errors, status: :unprocessable_entity
    end
  end

  # DELETE /api/users/1
  def destroy
    @user.destroy
  end

  private

  def set_user
    @user = User.find(params[:id])
  end

  def user_params
    params.require(:user).permit(:name, :email)
```

```
    end
end
```

Responding with JSON

In the controller actions, we use `render json: ...` to respond with JSON data. Rails automatically serializes the data to JSON using the defined attributes of the model.

Testing API Endpoints

To test your API endpoints, you can use tools like `curl`, Postman, or write automated tests using libraries like RSpec or MiniTest. Writing tests ensures that your API behaves as expected and helps catch bugs early in the development process.

In the next section, we'll explore authentication and how to secure your API endpoints to protect sensitive data and actions.

9.3 Securing Your API with Authentication

Securing your API is a critical aspect of building robust web applications. You want to ensure that only authorized users or applications can access sensitive data and perform certain actions. In this section, we'll explore various authentication mechanisms you can use to secure your Ruby on Rails API.

1. Token-Based Authentication

Token-based authentication is a popular method for securing APIs. In this approach, a unique token is generated for each user upon login. This token is then sent with each API request in the request headers. The server validates the token, allowing access only to authenticated users.

To implement token-based authentication in Rails, you can use gems like `Devise Token Auth` or `JWT (JSON Web Tokens)` with `Knock`. These gems provide the necessary infrastructure to handle token authentication.

```
# Gemfile
gem 'devise_token_auth'
```

Once you've installed the gem, you can configure it in your application. It enables you to sign up, sign in, and authenticate users using tokens.

2. OAuth 2.0

OAuth 2.0 is a protocol that allows secure authorization between applications. It's commonly used for third-party authorization, such as allowing users to log in with their Google or Facebook accounts. In a Rails application, you can use the `Doorkeeper` gem to implement OAuth 2.0.

```
# Gemfile
gem 'doorkeeper'
```

With Doorkeeper, you can create OAuth 2.0 providers and consumers, enabling secure access to your API.

3. API Keys

API keys are simple but effective for authenticating users or applications. You generate a unique API key for each authorized entity, and it's sent with each API request. The server checks the API key's validity before processing the request.

To implement API key authentication in Rails, you can create a middleware or use gems like api_key or rack-api-key.

```
# app/middleware/api_key_authentication.rb
class ApiKeyAuthentication
  def initialize(app)
    @app = app
  end

  def call(env)
    api_key = env['HTTP_X_API_KEY']
    user = User.find_by(api_key: api_key)

    if user
      env['api.user'] = user
      @app.call(env)
    else
      [401, { 'Content-Type' => 'text/plain' }, ['Unauthorized']]
    end
  end
end
```

4. JWT (JSON Web Tokens)

JWT is a compact and self-contained way to securely transmit information between parties as a JSON object. It's commonly used for authentication and is easy to implement in Rails using the jwt gem.

```
# Gemfile
gem 'jwt'
```

JWTs consist of three parts: the header, payload, and signature. The server signs the token with a secret key, and the client sends it with each request. The server can then verify the token's authenticity and extract information from it.

Choosing the right authentication method depends on your application's requirements and use cases. Ensure that you follow security best practices and protect sensitive user data when implementing authentication in your Ruby on Rails API.

9.4 Versioning Your API

As your Ruby on Rails application evolves, you may need to make changes to your API. These changes can include adding new features, modifying existing endpoints, or deprecating outdated functionality. To manage these changes effectively and ensure that your API remains stable for existing clients, versioning your API is essential.

Why API Versioning?

API versioning allows you to make backward-incompatible changes to your API while still supporting older clients that rely on previous versions. Without versioning, any changes you make to your API could potentially break existing client applications, leading to compatibility issues.

1. URI Versioning

One common way to version your API is through the URI (Uniform Resource Identifier). In URI versioning, the version number is included in the URL, typically as part of the path.

```ruby
# config/routes.rb
namespace :api do
  namespace :v1 do
    resources :products
  end
end
```

In this example, the v1 namespace indicates the API version, and the client can access the API by making requests to /api/v1/products. When you need to introduce breaking changes, you can create a new version, such as v2, and update the routes accordingly.

2. Accept Header Versioning

Another approach is to use the Accept header in the HTTP request to specify the desired API version. This approach is more RESTful, and it allows clients to request a specific version when making a request.

```ruby
# config/routes.rb
namespace :api, defaults: { format: 'json' } do
  resources :products, defaults: { format: 'json' }
end
```

In this configuration, the defaults option ensures that the API returns JSON by default. Clients can specify the desired version in the Accept header, like Accept: application/vnd.myapp.v1+json.

3. Subdomain Versioning

Subdomain versioning involves placing the version number in the subdomain of the URL. This approach is less common but can be useful in certain scenarios.

```ruby
# config/routes.rb
constraints subdomain: 'v1' do
  namespace :api do
    resources :products
  end
end
```

With subdomain versioning, clients access the API using a subdomain like `v1.api.example.com`.

4. Request Parameter Versioning

You can also include the version as a request parameter, although this approach is less conventional.

```ruby
# config/routes.rb
namespace :api do
  resources :products
end
```

Clients can specify the version in the URL, such as `/api/products?v=1`.

Handling Multiple Versions

When implementing API versioning, it's important to consider how to handle multiple versions in your codebase. You may need to create separate controllers or add conditional logic based on the requested version to ensure that the correct behavior is provided for each version.

In conclusion, API versioning is a crucial aspect of API design and maintenance. It allows you to make necessary changes and improvements to your API while ensuring compatibility with existing clients. Choose the versioning strategy that best fits your application's needs and communicate versioning changes clearly to your API consumers.

9.5 Documenting Your API with Swagger

Documentation is a critical aspect of building and maintaining a successful API. It helps developers understand how to use your API effectively, reduces confusion, and encourages adoption. Swagger is a popular tool that simplifies the process of documenting your Ruby on Rails API.

What is Swagger?

Swagger is an open-source framework for designing, building, and documenting RESTful APIs. It provides a suite of tools that allow you to generate interactive documentation, client SDKs, and even perform API testing directly from your API specification.

Getting Started with Swagger in Ruby on Rails

To start documenting your Ruby on Rails API using Swagger, you can follow these steps:

1. **Add Swagger to Your Gemfile**: First, add the `swagger-docs` gem to your Gemfile and run `bundle install`.

   ```
   gem 'swagger-docs'
   ```

2. **Generate Swagger Configuration**: Run the following command to generate the Swagger configuration file.

   ```
   rails generate swagger:install
   ```

   This command creates an initializer file (`config/initializers/swagger_docs.rb`) where you can configure your API documentation settings.

3. **Document Your API**: To document your API, add Swagger annotations to your controller actions and models. For example:

   ```
   # app/controllers/api/v1/products_controller.rb
   class Api::V1::ProductsController < ApplicationController
     # ...

     swagger_controller :products, 'Products Management'

     swagger_api :index do
       summary 'Fetches all products'
       param :query, :page, :integer, :optional, 'Page number'
       response :ok
     end

     # ...
   end
   ```

   Here, we've added Swagger annotations to the `index` action of the `ProductsController` to describe its behavior.

4. **Generate Swagger Documentation**: Use the following command to generate the Swagger documentation:

   ```
   rake swagger:docs:generate
   ```

   This command generates JSON and YAML files in the `public/swagger_docs` directory.

5. **Access Swagger UI**: You can now access the Swagger UI by visiting `/swagger/dist/index.html`. This interface allows developers to explore and test your API interactively.

6. **Customize Swagger UI (Optional)**: You can customize the appearance and behavior of the Swagger UI by modifying the Swagger UI configuration file located at `public/swagger_ui/configuration/uiConfiguration.json`.

Swagger UI Features

Swagger UI provides several features for API documentation:

- **Interactive API Exploration**: Developers can browse your API's endpoints, view parameters, and send test requests directly from the UI.

- **Auto-Generated API Client SDKs**: Swagger can generate client SDKs in multiple programming languages based on your API specification.

- **API Testing**: You can use Swagger UI to test your API by sending requests and viewing responses.

- **Documentation Generation**: Swagger automatically generates API documentation in JSON and YAML formats, which can be shared with other developers.

Conclusion

Swagger is a powerful tool for documenting your Ruby on Rails API. By adding Swagger annotations to your code and generating interactive documentation, you can make it easier for developers to understand and use your API effectively. Good documentation is a key factor in promoting your API and encouraging its adoption.

Chapter 10: Deploying Your Rails Application

Section 10.1: Preparing for Deployment

Deployment is a crucial phase in the development lifecycle of a Ruby on Rails application. It involves making your application accessible to users on the internet. Before you start deploying, there are several essential steps to consider.

1. Review and Optimize Your Code

Before deployment, it's essential to review your code thoroughly. Look for any potential bottlenecks, inefficiencies, or security vulnerabilities. Optimize database queries and ensure your application follows best practices.

2. Environment Configuration

Ensure that your application's environment settings are properly configured for production. This includes database configurations, secret keys, and any other environment-specific variables.

```
# config/environments/production.rb
config.action_mailer.default_url_options = { host: 'your-production-domain.co
m' }
```

3. Database Backup

Take a backup of your production database. This step is crucial to prevent data loss during deployment. Rails provides tools like pg_dump for PostgreSQL and mysqldump for MySQL to create backups.

4. Choose a Hosting Provider

Selecting the right hosting provider is a significant decision. Popular options for hosting Rails applications include Heroku, AWS, DigitalOcean, and many others. Consider factors like scalability, performance, and cost when making your choice.

5. Web Server Setup

Decide on a web server to serve your Rails application. Common choices include Nginx and Apache. Configure the web server to proxy requests to your Rails app using Passenger, Puma, or another application server.

```
# Example Nginx configuration
server {
    listen 80;
    server_name your-production-domain.com;
    root /path/to/your/app/public;

    location / {
        proxy_pass http://localhost:3000; # Assuming your app runs on port 30
00
    }
}
```

6. SSL Certificate

If your application deals with sensitive data or user authentication, consider securing it with an SSL certificate. This ensures data encryption between your server and users' browsers.

7. Continuous Integration and Deployment (CI/CD)

Implement CI/CD pipelines to automate deployment. Tools like Jenkins, CircleCI, or GitHub Actions can help you build, test, and deploy your app whenever changes are pushed to your version control repository.

8. Monitoring and Error Tracking

Set up monitoring tools to track your application's performance and catch errors. Services like New Relic, Sentry, and Datadog can provide insights into how your application behaves in production.

9. Scaling Plan

Plan for scaling your application as traffic grows. Decide whether you'll use horizontal scaling (adding more servers) or vertical scaling (upgrading server resources). Services like AWS Elastic Beanstalk and Heroku make scaling easier.

10. Backup and Recovery

Implement a backup and recovery strategy for your production data. Regularly back up your databases and files to ensure you can quickly recover from data loss or server failures.

11. Deployment Checklist

Create a deployment checklist that includes all the necessary steps and configurations. Use this checklist to ensure consistency and avoid missing crucial tasks during deployment.

12. Testing in Production

Before opening your application to the public, perform thorough testing in a production-like environment. This helps identify and fix any issues that may arise only in the production environment.

Deployment can be a complex process, but with careful planning and the right tools, you can ensure a smooth transition from development to production. In the subsequent sections of this chapter, we'll dive deeper into various aspects of deployment, including choosing a hosting provider, setting up a production environment, deploying with tools like Capistrano, and strategies for scaling and monitoring your Rails app.

Section 10.2: Choosing a Hosting Provider

Choosing the right hosting provider for your Ruby on Rails application is a critical decision that can impact your app's performance, scalability, and cost. Each hosting provider offers a range of services and features, so it's important to evaluate your options carefully.

1. Heroku

Heroku is a popular Platform as a Service (PaaS) provider that simplifies the deployment process. It offers a wide range of add-ons and a simple interface for managing your Rails application. Heroku abstracts many infrastructure concerns, making it an excellent choice for smaller projects and startups. However, it may become expensive for large-scale applications.

- Easy to set up and deploy.
- Supports automatic scaling.
- Provides a wide range of add-ons, including databases and caching services.
- Offers a free tier for small projects.

Cons:

- Limited customization of infrastructure.
- Can be costly as your app scales.
- Limited control over the underlying server environment.

2. AWS (Amazon Web Services)

Amazon Web Services (AWS) is one of the most widely used cloud computing platforms. AWS provides a range of services, including Elastic Beanstalk for deploying Rails applications. It offers extensive scalability and customization options.

Pros:

- Highly customizable infrastructure.
- Scalable and cost-effective.
- Offers various database options.
- Suitable for a wide range of application sizes.

Cons:

- Steeper learning curve compared to PaaS providers.
- Requires more configuration and management.

3. DigitalOcean

DigitalOcean is known for its simplicity and developer-friendly approach. It offers virtual private servers (Droplets) that you can configure according to your needs. DigitalOcean provides a straightforward way to set up and deploy Rails applications.

Pros:

- Developer-friendly with straightforward setup.
- Affordable pricing.
- Customizable virtual servers.
- Good documentation and community support.

Cons:

- You need to manage infrastructure yourself.
- Limited automatic scaling options.

4. Google Cloud Platform (GCP)

Google Cloud Platform (GCP) offers a range of services for hosting Rails applications. Google App Engine and Google Kubernetes Engine (GKE) are suitable options for deploying and managing Rails apps.

Pros:
- Scalable and flexible.
- Strong focus on machine learning and data services.
- Good integration with other Google Cloud services.

Cons:
- Can be complex to set up for beginners.
- Pricing can be higher compared to some other providers.

5. Microsoft Azure

Microsoft Azure is Microsoft's cloud computing platform. It provides services for hosting Rails applications, including Azure App Service. Azure is a good choice if you're already invested in the Microsoft ecosystem.

Pros:
- Integration with other Microsoft products.
- Supports multiple programming languages.
- Scalable and reliable.

Cons:
- Some features may be more oriented toward .NET applications.
- Pricing can vary depending on the services used.

6. Other Options

There are several other hosting providers to consider, such as Linode, Vultr, and IBM Cloud. Each provider has its own strengths and weaknesses, so it's important to evaluate them based on your specific requirements and budget.

Conclusion

Choosing the right hosting provider depends on your application's size, complexity, and your level of expertise. Consider factors like scalability, cost, customization, and the level of control you require. It's also a good practice to review each provider's pricing structure to ensure it aligns with your budget. Ultimately, the hosting provider you choose should support your Rails application's growth and performance needs.

Section 10.3: Setting Up Production Environment

Setting up a production environment for your Ruby on Rails application is a crucial step in the deployment process. A production environment is where your application will run for real users, so it must be configured securely and efficiently. In this section, we'll discuss the key considerations and steps involved in setting up a production environment for your Rails app.

1. Web Server Configuration

Nginx or Apache

One of the first decisions you'll make is choosing a web server to serve your Rails application. Two popular choices are Nginx and Apache. These web servers can act as reverse proxies, forwarding incoming requests to your Rails application server (usually Puma or Unicorn). You'll need to configure the web server to handle SSL/TLS, load balancing, and other important aspects of web hosting.

```
# Example Nginx configuration for a Rails app
server {
    listen 80;
    server_name example.com www.example.com;
    location / {
        proxy_pass http://localhost:3000; # Forward requests to your Rails ap
p
    }
}
```

SSL/TLS Configuration

It's essential to secure your production environment with SSL/TLS encryption. You can obtain SSL certificates from certificate authorities like Let's Encrypt or commercial providers. Configure your web server to enable HTTPS for secure data transmission.

2. Application Server

You'll need an application server to run your Ruby on Rails application. Popular choices include Puma and Unicorn. These servers handle incoming HTTP requests, manage multiple application processes, and provide load balancing.

```
# Example Puma configuration file (config/puma.rb)
workers 2
threads 1, 6
bind 'unix:///path/to/socket.sock'
```

3. Database Setup

In a production environment, you should use a robust database system like PostgreSQL or MySQL. Configure your Rails application to use the production database and set up database backups and maintenance tasks.

```
# Example database.yml configuration
production:
  adapter: postgresql
  encoding: unicode
  database: myapp_production
  pool: 5
  username: myapp_user
  password: <%= ENV['MYAPP_DATABASE_PASSWORD'] %>
```

4. Environment Variables

Manage sensitive configuration data, such as database credentials and API keys, using environment variables. This practice enhances security and allows you to change configurations without modifying your code.

```
export SECRET_KEY_BASE=your_secret_key
export DATABASE_URL=your_database_url
```

5. Monitoring and Logging

Implement monitoring solutions like New Relic or Datadog to track your application's performance, error rates, and resource usage. Configure log management to collect and analyze logs for debugging and auditing.

6. Deployment Scripts

Automate your deployment process with deployment scripts or tools like Capistrano. These scripts ensure a smooth and consistent deployment workflow.

7. Scaling

Plan for scalability by setting up load balancing and considering containerization with tools like Docker. Cloud providers offer auto-scaling options that can handle traffic spikes.

Conclusion

Setting up a production environment for your Ruby on Rails application requires careful planning and consideration of security, performance, and scalability. By following best practices and utilizing the right tools and configurations, you can ensure that your application is well-prepared to serve real users in a reliable and secure manner.

Section 10.4: Deploying with Capistrano

Capistrano is a popular deployment automation tool that streamlines the deployment process of Ruby on Rails applications. It allows you to deploy your application code to multiple servers with minimal downtime and provides a consistent and repeatable deployment workflow. In this section, we'll explore how to set up Capistrano for deploying your Rails application.

Installation

First, you'll need to add Capistrano to your Rails project's Gemfile:

```
# Gemfile
group :development do
  gem 'capistrano', '~> 3.14'
  gem 'capistrano-rails', '~> 1.7'
  gem 'capistrano-bundler', '~> 2.1'
  gem 'capistrano3-puma', '~> 5.0' # If you're using Puma
end
```

Then, run `bundle install` to install the Capistrano-related gems.

Configuration

Generate the necessary Capistrano configuration files using the following command:

```
cap install
```

This will create several files in the `config/deploy` directory of your Rails application, including `deploy.rb` and `production.rb`.

In `config/deploy.rb`, you can configure various settings such as the application name, repository URL, deployment path, and more:

```
# config/deploy.rb
set :application, 'your_app_name'
set :repo_url, 'git@example.com:your/repo.git'
set :deploy_to, '/var/www/your_app_name'
```

In `config/deploy/production.rb`, specify the server(s) where your application will be deployed:

```
# config/deploy/production.rb
server 'your_server_ip', user: 'deploy', roles: %w{app db web}
```

Deploying Your Application

To deploy your Rails application using Capistrano, run the following command:

```
cap production deploy
```

Capistrano will perform the following tasks:

1. Clone the Git repository on the server.
2. Create a new release directory for the deployment.
3. Install necessary gems using Bundler.
4. Run database migrations.
5. Precompile assets.
6. Restart the application server (Puma, Unicorn, etc.).

Custom Tasks

You can define custom Capistrano tasks in your Rails project's `lib/capistrano/tasks` directory. These tasks can be used to perform additional actions during deployment, such as clearing caches, sending notifications, or any other specific tasks related to your application.

Rollbacks

Capistrano also provides the ability to perform rollbacks in case of deployment issues. You can rollback to a previous release using the following command:

```
cap production deploy:rollback
```

Conclusion

Capistrano simplifies the deployment process for Ruby on Rails applications and ensures a consistent and reliable deployment workflow. By following the installation and configuration steps outlined in this section, you can effectively deploy your Rails application to production environments with ease.

Section 10.5: Scaling and Monitoring Your Rails App

Scalability and monitoring are critical aspects of deploying and maintaining a Ruby on Rails application. As your application grows and attracts more users, you'll need to ensure that it can handle increased traffic and monitor its performance to identify and address potential issues. In this section, we'll discuss strategies for scaling your Rails app and monitoring its health.

Scaling Your Rails Application

Horizontal Scaling

Horizontal scaling involves adding more servers to your application's infrastructure to distribute the incoming traffic. This can be achieved using load balancers, which evenly distribute requests among multiple application servers. Popular load balancing solutions include NGINX and HAProxy.

To set up horizontal scaling with NGINX, you can configure it to proxy requests to multiple application server instances. Here's a simplified NGINX configuration snippet:

```
upstream rails_servers {
  server app_server1:3000;
  server app_server2:3000;
}

server {
  listen 80;
  server_name your_domain.com;

  location / {
    proxy_pass http://rails_servers;
    # Additional NGINX configurations...
  }
}
```

Database Scaling

Scaling the database is often a bottleneck in Rails applications. You can consider strategies like:

- **Replication:** Use database replication to distribute read-heavy traffic across multiple database servers.
- **Sharding:** Sharding involves partitioning your database into smaller, manageable parts.
- **Caching:** Implement caching mechanisms like Redis or Memcached to reduce the database load.

Monitoring Your Rails Application

Application Performance Monitoring (APM)

APM tools like New Relic and AppDynamics provide detailed insights into your application's performance. They can help you identify slow database queries, bottlenecks, and other performance issues.

Log Aggregation

Centralized log aggregation tools like ELK Stack (Elasticsearch, Logstash, Kibana) or cloud-based services like Papertrail can collect and analyze logs from all parts of your application, making it easier to detect and troubleshoot errors.

Error Tracking

Error tracking services like Sentry and Rollbar automatically capture and report errors in your application code. They provide detailed error reports, including stack traces, making it easier to identify and fix issues.

Infrastructure Monitoring

Tools like Prometheus and Grafana allow you to monitor server and infrastructure metrics, such as CPU usage, memory usage, and network traffic. This helps ensure that your servers are healthy and performing optimally.

Autoscaling

Autoscaling allows your application to automatically add or remove servers based on traffic demand. Cloud providers like AWS, Google Cloud, and Azure offer autoscaling features that can be configured to ensure your application scales seamlessly.

Load Testing

Perform load testing using tools like Apache JMeter or Locust to simulate heavy traffic on your application. This helps you identify performance bottlenecks and ensures that your application can handle increased loads.

Conclusion

Scaling and monitoring are continuous processes that require ongoing attention as your Ruby on Rails application evolves. By implementing the strategies and tools discussed in this section, you can ensure that your application remains performant, reliable, and capable of handling increased traffic and user demand.

Chapter 11: Performance Optimization

Performance optimization is a crucial aspect of web application development, especially when working with Ruby on Rails. In this chapter, we will explore various strategies and techniques for improving the performance of your Rails applications. From identifying bottlenecks to implementing caching and load balancing, we'll cover essential topics to make your Rails app faster and more efficient.

Section 11.1: Identifying Performance Bottlenecks

Performance bottlenecks can significantly impact the responsiveness of your Rails application. Identifying and addressing these bottlenecks is the first step in optimization.

Monitoring and Profiling

To pinpoint performance issues, you can use tools like Rails' built-in performance monitoring features, which provide detailed information about the execution time of different parts of your application. Additionally, external tools like New Relic and AppDynamics offer comprehensive application performance monitoring (APM) solutions.

Common Bottlenecks

Some common performance bottlenecks in Rails applications include:

- **Database Queries:** Slow database queries can significantly affect your application's performance. Use tools like Bullet to identify N+1 query problems and optimize your queries.

- **View Rendering:** Complex views with many partials or unnecessary calculations can slow down your application. Optimize views by minimizing the use of partials and reducing unnecessary logic.

- **Asset Loading:** Large assets like JavaScript and CSS files can increase page load times. Implement asset optimization techniques, including asset minification and compression.

- **Inefficient Code:** Identify and refactor inefficient code in your controllers, models, and views. Profiling tools like Rack Mini Profiler can help you find areas that need improvement.

Section 11.2: Caching Strategies in Rails

Caching is an effective way to reduce the load on your application and improve response times. In this section, we'll explore various caching strategies in Rails.

Page Caching

Page caching involves saving the HTML output of a page and serving it directly from storage without invoking Rails or the database. This is ideal for static or infrequently changing pages. Rails provides built-in support for page caching.

Action Caching

Action caching is similar to page caching but allows caching at the controller action level. It's useful for pages with dynamic content that doesn't change frequently. You can enable action caching with the `caches_action` method.

Fragment Caching

Fragment caching involves caching specific parts of a page, such as a sidebar or a complex view component. Use the `cache` helper to wrap the code you want to cache.

Key-Based Caching

Key-based caching lets you cache data with a unique key. When the data changes, you can expire or update the cache using the key. This is common when caching database query results or API responses.

Caching Stores

Rails supports various caching stores, including memory-based stores like Memcached and Redis, and file-based stores. Choose the appropriate caching store based on your application's needs and scalability requirements.

Section 11.3: Database Optimization Techniques

The database is often a performance bottleneck in Rails applications. Optimizing your database queries and schema can significantly improve application speed.

Indexing

Properly indexing your database tables can dramatically speed up query execution. Identify columns frequently used in queries and create indexes for them.

Database Migrations

Optimize your database schema by reviewing and improving your database migrations. Avoid unnecessary columns and indexes.

Query Optimization

Use the EXPLAIN command to analyze the execution plan of your queries. Optimize slow queries by adding indexes, rewriting queries, or using database-specific optimizations.

Connection Pooling

Configure the connection pool size in your database configuration to ensure efficient database connections and prevent resource exhaustion.

Section 11.4: Load Balancing and Scaling

As your application grows, load balancing and scaling become essential to handle increased traffic. Load balancing distributes incoming requests among multiple servers, while scaling involves adding more resources to your infrastructure.

Load Balancers

Implement a load balancer to distribute requests across multiple application server instances. NGINX and HAProxy are popular choices for load balancing.

Horizontal Scaling

Scale your application horizontally by adding more application server instances. This approach allows your application to handle increased traffic and provides redundancy.

Vertical Scaling

Vertical scaling involves increasing the resources of a single server, such as upgrading CPU, memory, or storage. While vertical scaling has its limits, it can be a quick solution for handling increased loads.

Section 11.5: Profiling and Benchmarking Your Application

Profiling and benchmarking tools help you measure and analyze your application's performance under different scenarios.

Ruby Profiling

Tools like StackProf and rbtrace provide insights into your application's code execution, helping you identify bottlenecks and performance issues.

Benchmarking

Use benchmarking tools like wrk and Apache Benchmark (ab) to simulate and measure the performance of your application under load.

Continuous Performance Testing

Incorporate performance testing into your continuous integration and deployment pipeline. Tools like Travis CI and Jenkins can

Chapter 11: Performance Optimization

Performance optimization is a critical aspect of web application development, especially when working with Ruby on Rails. In this chapter, we will explore various strategies and techniques for improving the performance of your Rails applications. From identifying bottlenecks to implementing caching and load balancing, we'll cover essential topics to make your Rails app faster and more efficient.

Section 11.1: Identifying Performance Bottlenecks

Performance bottlenecks can significantly impact the responsiveness of your Rails application. Identifying and addressing these bottlenecks is the first step in optimization.

Monitoring and Profiling

To pinpoint performance issues, you can use tools like Rails' built-in performance monitoring features, which provide detailed information about the execution time of different parts of your application. Additionally, external tools like New Relic and AppDynamics offer comprehensive application performance monitoring (APM) solutions.

Common Bottlenecks

Some common performance bottlenecks in Rails applications include:

- **Database Queries:** Slow database queries can significantly affect your application's performance. Use tools like Bullet to identify N+1 query problems and optimize your queries.

- **View Rendering:** Complex views with many partials or unnecessary calculations can slow down your application. Optimize views by minimizing the use of partials and reducing unnecessary logic.

- **Asset Loading:** Large assets like JavaScript and CSS files can increase page load times. Implement asset optimization techniques, including asset minification and compression.

- **Inefficient Code:** Identify and refactor inefficient code in your controllers, models, and views. Profiling tools like Rack Mini Profiler can help you find areas that need improvement.

Example: Identifying N+1 Query Problems

```ruby
# Inefficient Code (N+1 Query)
@posts = Post.all
@posts.each do |post|
  puts post.comments.count
end
```

```
# Efficient Code (Eager Loading)
@posts = Post.includes(:comments)
@posts.each do |post|
  puts post.comments.count
end
```

In the example above, the inefficient code leads to an N+1 query problem, where a separate query is executed for each post's comments. The efficient code uses eager loading to fetch all comments in a single query, improving performance.

Identifying and addressing N+1 query problems is just one aspect of performance optimization. Monitoring and profiling your application will reveal other areas that require improvement.

Section 11.2: Caching Strategies in Rails

Caching is a powerful technique to improve the performance and responsiveness of your Ruby on Rails application. It involves storing frequently accessed data or rendered views so that subsequent requests can be served more quickly. In this section, we will explore various caching strategies available in Rails.

1. Page Caching

Page caching is the simplest form of caching in Rails. It involves storing the entire HTML output of a page so that it can be served directly without going through the Rails application stack. Page caching is suitable for pages that are mostly static and don't rely on user-specific data.

To enable page caching in Rails, you can use the `caches_page` method in your controller:

```
class PagesController < ApplicationController
  caches_page :home
  # ...
end
```

This caches the `home` action, and subsequent requests to the same page will be served from the cache.

2. Action Caching

Action caching is similar to page caching but allows you to cache specific actions within a controller. It's useful when you want to cache parts of a page while keeping some parts dynamic. Action caching caches the rendered view of an action and is more flexible than page caching.

You can enable action caching like this:

```
class ProductsController < ApplicationController
  caches_action :show
```

```
  # ...
end
```

3. Fragment Caching

Fragment caching allows you to cache specific parts or fragments of a view. This is handy when you have a dynamic page with some parts that can be cached independently. You can use the `cache` helper in your views to define what to cache:

```
<% cache("product_#{product.id}_details") do %>
  <div class="product-details">
    <!-- Render product details here -->
  </div>
<% end %>
```

4. Model Caching

Model caching involves caching the results of database queries. Rails provides built-in support for caching model objects and associations. For example, you can cache a user's posts like this:

```
class User < ApplicationRecord
  has_many :posts, -> { includes(:comments) }, cached: true
  # ...
end
```

This caches the user's posts and their associated comments, reducing the number of database queries.

5. HTTP Caching

HTTP caching involves setting appropriate HTTP headers to allow browsers and proxies to cache responses. Rails provides mechanisms like the `stale?` and `fresh_when` methods to control HTTP caching in your controllers.

```
class ProductsController < ApplicationController
  def show
    @product = Product.find(params[:id])
    fresh_when(@product)
  end
end
```

These are some of the caching strategies available in Rails. Effective caching can significantly boost the performance of your application, but it should be used judiciously, considering the nature of your content and the trade-offs between performance and freshness.

Section 11.3: Database Optimization Techniques

Database optimization is a critical aspect of ensuring your Ruby on Rails application performs efficiently and responds quickly to user requests. In this section, we'll explore several techniques to optimize your database for better performance.

1. Indexing

Indexes are data structures that improve the speed of data retrieval operations on database tables. By creating indexes on columns commonly used in search or filtering operations, you can significantly reduce query execution times. In Rails migrations, you can add indexes like this:

```ruby
class AddIndexToUsersEmail < ActiveRecord::Migration[6.0]
  def change
    add_index :users, :email, unique: true
  end
end
```

2. Query Optimization

Efficient query design is crucial for database performance. ActiveRecord, Rails' default ORM (Object-Relational Mapping) library, generates SQL queries for you, but you should always review and optimize complex queries. Use tools like the `explain` method to analyze query execution plans and identify bottlenecks:

```ruby
User.where(status: 'active').explain
```

3. Database Connection Pooling

Database connection pooling helps manage and reuse database connections efficiently. In Rails, this is configured in the database.yml file. Adjust the `pool` setting according to your application's needs to prevent resource exhaustion and delays due to database connection establishment.

```yaml
development:
  adapter: postgresql
  database: myapp_development
  pool: 5
  ...
```

4. Avoid N+1 Query Problem

The N+1 query problem occurs when you load a parent record along with its associated child records, resulting in additional queries for each child record. Use ActiveRecord's `includes` or `eager_load` methods to load associations eagerly and prevent the N+1 query problem:

```
# N+1 query without eager loading
@posts = Post.all
@posts.each { |post| puts post.comments.count }  # N queries

# Eager loading to prevent N+1 query
@posts = Post.includes(:comments).all
@posts.each { |post| puts post.comments.count }  # 1 query
```

5. Database Sharding

Database sharding involves distributing your database across multiple servers or instances. It can be an effective way to scale your application when dealing with a large amount of data. Rails doesn't provide built-in sharding support, but there are gems and libraries available for implementing sharding strategies.

6. Use Caching

Caching is not limited to application-level caching; you can also cache database queries and query results. Libraries like `dalli` for Memcached or `redis-rails` for Redis integration can help you implement query caching easily.

7. Regular Maintenance

Regular database maintenance is essential to keep your database in good health. Perform tasks like vacuuming and optimizing tables to free up space and keep indexes efficient. Automate these tasks using tools provided by your database system (e.g., PostgreSQL's `vacuumdb`).

These are some of the key techniques to optimize your database performance in a Ruby on Rails application. Always monitor your application's performance, profile your queries, and adjust your optimization strategies as needed to ensure your application runs smoothly as it scales.

Section 11.4: Load Balancing and Scaling

Scaling is an essential aspect of managing a Ruby on Rails application, especially as your user base grows. Load balancing is a key technique used to distribute incoming traffic across multiple application servers, ensuring optimal performance, high availability, and reliability. In this section, we'll explore load balancing and scaling strategies for Rails applications.

Load Balancing

Load balancing is the process of evenly distributing incoming web traffic or requests across multiple servers to prevent any single server from becoming a bottleneck. Load balancers can be implemented in various ways:

1. **Reverse Proxy**: A reverse proxy server, such as Nginx or Apache, can act as a load balancer. It receives incoming requests and forwards them to backend application servers based on predefined rules. Here's an example Nginx configuration:

```
upstream rails_servers {
  server app1.example.com;
  server app2.example.com;
  server app3.example.com;
}

server {
  listen 80;
  server_name myapp.com;

  location / {
    proxy_pass http://rails_servers;
    # Additional configuration options
  }
}
```

2. **Load Balancer Services**: Cloud providers like AWS, Google Cloud, and Azure offer load balancing services that can distribute traffic across multiple virtual machines or containers.

Horizontal Scaling

Horizontal scaling involves adding more application server instances to handle increased load. Rails applications can be horizontally scaled by deploying multiple identical instances behind a load balancer. Key considerations for horizontal scaling include:

- **Session Management**: When you scale horizontally, you need to ensure session data is accessible across all instances. You can use solutions like database-backed sessions or external session stores like Redis.

- **Database Scaling**: As traffic increases, your database might become a bottleneck. Consider using database replication, sharding, or managed database services to handle increased load.

- **Asset Storage**: If your application serves user-uploaded assets (e.g., images, files), use cloud-based storage solutions like Amazon S3 or Google Cloud Storage to ensure scalability.

Vertical Scaling

Vertical scaling involves upgrading individual server instances with more CPU, memory, or resources. While it can provide a performance boost, it has limitations and might not be as cost-effective as horizontal scaling. Key considerations for vertical scaling include:

- **Database Optimization**: Optimize your database performance by tuning configurations, adding more memory, and optimizing queries.

- **Web Server Optimization**: Fine-tune your web server (e.g., Nginx, Passenger, Puma) settings to handle increased traffic efficiently.

- **Caching**: Implement various caching strategies, such as page caching, fragment caching, and object caching, to reduce the load on your application servers.

- **Content Delivery Networks (CDNs)**: Use CDNs to cache and serve static assets closer to users, reducing the load on your application servers.

Auto-Scaling

Auto-scaling is a dynamic scaling approach where your infrastructure automatically adjusts the number of application instances based on traffic load. Cloud providers offer auto-scaling services that can automatically add or remove instances as needed. This ensures efficient resource utilization and cost savings.

Monitoring and Alerts

Regardless of your scaling strategy, monitoring your application's performance and setting up alerts for key metrics is crucial. Tools like New Relic, Datadog, and Prometheus can help you track server health, response times, and resource utilization.

In conclusion, load balancing and scaling are essential for ensuring the availability and performance of your Ruby on Rails application. Whether you choose horizontal scaling, vertical scaling, or a combination of both, monitoring and regular testing are critical to maintaining a robust and responsive application as it grows.

Section 11.5: Profiling and Benchmarking Your Application

Profiling and benchmarking are essential techniques for identifying and addressing performance bottlenecks in your Ruby on Rails application. These processes help you understand how your code and database queries perform, allowing you to optimize and fine-tune your application for better efficiency and user experience.

Profiling Your Rails Application

Profiling involves measuring the performance of your application and identifying specific areas where improvements can be made. Rails provides built-in tools and gems to help with profiling:

1. **Rails Profiler**: Rails comes with a built-in profiler that can be enabled by adding the ?profile=true query parameter to a URL while running your development server. This generates a detailed report highlighting the time spent in various parts of your application.

2. **Rack Mini Profiler**: The "rack-mini-profiler" gem is a popular choice for profiling. It offers real-time performance profiling directly within your web application,

displaying information about SQL queries, view rendering times, and more in the browser's developer console.

```
gem 'rack-mini-profiler', group: :development
```

3. **Bullet**: The "bullet" gem helps identify N+1 query problems in your code by notifying you when your application generates unnecessary database queries. It can be particularly useful for optimizing database interactions.

```
gem 'bullet', group: :development
```

4. **Ruby-Prof**: The "ruby-prof" gem provides detailed CPU profiling information for your Ruby code. It allows you to analyze which parts of your code consume the most CPU time.

```
gem 'ruby-prof', group: :development
```

Benchmarking Your Rails Application

Benchmarking involves running tests or simulations to evaluate the performance of your application under specific conditions. Here's how you can approach benchmarking in your Rails application:

1. **Apache Benchmark (ab)**: Apache Benchmark is a command-line tool that can be used to simulate multiple users accessing your application simultaneously. It provides metrics like requests per second, response time, and concurrency.

```
ab -n 1000 -c 10 http://localhost:3000/
```

2. **Wrk**: Wrk is another popular HTTP benchmarking tool that allows you to create complex scenarios for testing. It's highly configurable and provides detailed metrics.

```
wrk -t10 -c100 -d30s http://localhost:3000/
```

3. **Siege**: Siege is a simple, yet effective, benchmarking tool for HTTP requests. It allows you to specify the number of concurrent users and the duration of the test.

```
siege -c10 -t30s http://localhost:3000/
```

4. **JMeter**: Apache JMeter is a more advanced tool for load testing and benchmarking. It can simulate various types of HTTP requests and offers extensive reporting and analysis capabilities.

Interpreting Results

When profiling or benchmarking your application, pay attention to key metrics like response times, throughput, error rates, and resource utilization. Identify areas where performance is suboptimal, and use the collected data to make informed optimizations.

Optimization strategies may include database indexing, query optimization, code refactoring, caching, and horizontal or vertical scaling, as discussed in previous sections.

Remember that profiling and benchmarking are ongoing processes. Regularly monitor your application's performance, especially after implementing optimizations, to ensure that it continues to meet user expectations as it evolves.

In conclusion, profiling and benchmarking are valuable practices for maintaining a high-performing Ruby on Rails application. They empower you to identify and address performance bottlenecks, ultimately leading to a better user experience and efficient resource utilization.

Chapter 12: Security Best Practices

In today's digital landscape, web application security is of paramount importance. Ruby on Rails provides several built-in security features, but it's crucial for developers to be aware of common web application security threats and follow best practices to protect their applications and user data. This chapter explores various security topics and practices that are essential for building secure Ruby on Rails applications.

Section 12.1: Common Web Application Security Threats

Before delving into security best practices, it's vital to understand the common threats that web applications can face. Being aware of these threats allows you to proactively implement security measures. Here are some prevalent web application security threats:

1. Cross-Site Scripting (XSS)

Cross-Site Scripting is a vulnerability that allows attackers to inject malicious scripts into web pages viewed by other users. These scripts can steal sensitive data or manipulate the page's content.

Mitigation: Use output encoding and validation to prevent XSS attacks. Rails provides built-in protection through automatic escaping of user-generated content.

2. Cross-Site Request Forgery (CSRF)

CSRF attacks trick authenticated users into making unwanted requests without their consent. These attacks can lead to actions such as changing a user's password or making unauthorized transactions.

Mitigation: Rails includes built-in CSRF protection with the use of tokens in forms. Ensure that you're using these tokens correctly.

3. SQL Injection

SQL injection occurs when attackers insert malicious SQL queries into input fields, manipulating database operations. This can lead to unauthorized access or data loss.

Mitigation: Always use parameterized queries or ActiveRecord's query-building methods to prevent SQL injection. Avoid constructing SQL queries using user inputs directly.

4. Insecure Authentication

Weak or insecure authentication mechanisms can lead to unauthorized access to user accounts. This includes using weak passwords, not using encryption, or storing passwords in plaintext.

Mitigation: Implement strong password policies, use encryption (e.g., bcrypt) for password storage, and ensure secure session management.

5. Insecure File Uploads

Allowing users to upload files can be risky if not properly validated. Malicious files can be uploaded and executed on the server.

Mitigation: Implement strict file type validation and store uploaded files in a location that prevents direct execution.

6. Security Misconfigurations

Misconfigurations, such as exposing sensitive information in error messages or not updating dependencies, can create security vulnerabilities.

Mitigation: Regularly review and update dependencies, restrict error messages, and follow secure coding practices.

7. Lack of Session Management

Improper session management can lead to session fixation or hijacking, allowing attackers to impersonate users.

Mitigation: Use secure and random session tokens, regenerate tokens on login, and ensure session timeout.

8. Broken Authentication

Broken authentication vulnerabilities occur when authentication mechanisms are not correctly implemented, allowing attackers to bypass authentication or gain unauthorized access.

Mitigation: Test authentication thoroughly, use secure password recovery processes, and protect against brute-force attacks.

9. Data Exposure

Exposing sensitive data, such as passwords or payment information, due to improper data handling or encryption, is a significant security risk.

Mitigation: Implement strong data encryption, limit data exposure, and follow data protection regulations (e.g., GDPR).

10. Unvalidated Redirects and Forwards

Unvalidated redirects and forwards can lead to phishing attacks, where users are redirected to malicious websites.

Mitigation: Always validate and sanitize redirect and forward URLs, and avoid using user-generated input for redirection.

Understanding these common threats is the first step in building secure Ruby on Rails applications. In the subsequent sections of this chapter, we'll explore specific security practices and techniques to mitigate these risks effectively.

Section 12.2: Cross-Site Scripting (XSS) Protection

Cross-Site Scripting (XSS) is a severe security vulnerability that occurs when an attacker injects malicious scripts into web pages viewed by other users. These scripts can steal sensitive data or manipulate the page's content, potentially harming users and your application's reputation. In this section, we'll explore how to protect your Ruby on Rails application against XSS attacks.

1. Output Encoding

One of the fundamental ways to mitigate XSS attacks in Rails is through proper output encoding. Rails provides automatic escaping of user-generated content by default, which means that any data output to the HTML page is escaped to prevent script execution. This feature helps protect your application against most XSS vulnerabilities.

For example, if you have user-generated content displayed in your view using ERB templates:

```
<%= user_input %>
```

Rails will automatically escape the `user_input`, rendering any potentially harmful script harmless.

2. Whitelisting and Sanitization

In some cases, you might need to allow certain HTML tags or attributes in user-generated content. Rails provides a `sanitize` helper method that allows you to define a whitelist of allowed HTML elements and attributes while still escaping potentially harmful content.

```
<%= sanitize(user_input, tags: %w(strong em), attributes: %w(href)) %>
```

This example allows the `strong` and `em` tags and the `href` attribute while escaping all other content.

3. Content Security Policy (CSP)

Content Security Policy is an additional layer of security that helps protect your application from XSS attacks. CSP allows you to specify which sources of content are trusted and which are not. If an attacker tries to inject scripts from an untrusted source, the browser will block them from executing.

You can set up a Content Security Policy in your Rails application's configuration:

```
# config/application.rb
```

```
config.action_dispatch.default_headers = {
  'Content-Security-Policy' => "default-src 'self' https://trusted-cdn.com; s
cript-src 'self' 'unsafe-inline' 'unsafe-eval' https://trusted-scripts.com;"
}
```

In this example, we're allowing scripts to be loaded only from the same origin ('self'), a trusted CDN (https://trusted-cdn.com), and specific trusted script sources (https://trusted-scripts.com).

4. Escaping JavaScript

When including user-generated content within JavaScript, it's essential to properly escape it. Rails provides the escape_javascript helper for this purpose:

```
var user_input = "<%= j(user_input) %>";
```

The j method ensures that the user input is escaped correctly for JavaScript context.

5. Reflected and Stored XSS

Be aware that XSS attacks can be both reflected (executed immediately) and stored (persisted and executed later). For stored XSS, validate and sanitize user input when storing data in the database and when rendering it.

By following these best practices, you can significantly reduce the risk of XSS vulnerabilities in your Ruby on Rails application. It's essential to stay vigilant and regularly review and test your application for security issues, as new attack vectors may emerge over time.

Section 12.3: Cross-Site Request Forgery (CSRF) Prevention

Cross-Site Request Forgery (CSRF) is another common web application security threat. It occurs when an attacker tricks a user into performing unintended actions on a different website, often without their knowledge or consent. In this section, we'll explore how to protect your Ruby on Rails application against CSRF attacks.

1. Rails CSRF Protection

Rails includes built-in CSRF protection to mitigate this threat. CSRF protection relies on the use of an authenticity token, which is embedded in forms and requests. When a user submits a form, Rails checks if the authenticity token in the request matches the one expected for the session. If they don't match, the request is considered fraudulent, and Rails will reject it.

To enable CSRF protection, ensure that the protect_from_forgery method is called in your ApplicationController:

```ruby
# app/controllers/application_controller.rb

class ApplicationController < ActionController::Base
  protect_from_forgery with: :exception
end
```

By default, Rails will include the authenticity token in forms created using the `form_for` and `form_tag` helpers.

2. Handling Ajax Requests

When making AJAX requests to your Rails application, it's essential to include the CSRF token explicitly. You can do this by setting the `X-CSRF-Token` header in your AJAX requests or including the token as a parameter.

Header-based approach (using jQuery):
```javascript
$.ajax({
  url: '/your_ajax_endpoint',
  type: 'POST',
  headers: {
    'X-CSRF-Token': $('meta[name="csrf-token"]').attr('content')
  },
  // other options
});
```

Parameter-based approach (using Rails UJS):
```
# In your view file
<%= javascript_include_tag :defaults %>

# In your JavaScript code
$.ajax({
  url: '/your_ajax_endpoint',
  type: 'POST',
  data: {
    authenticity_token: $('meta[name="csrf-token"]').attr('content')
    // other parameters
  },
  // other options
});
```

Ensure that you have the following meta tag in the `<head>` section of your layout:

```html
<meta name="csrf-token" content="<%= form_authenticity_token %>">
```

This meta tag provides the CSRF token to your JavaScript code.

3. Same-Site Cookies

You can enhance CSRF protection by setting the `SameSite` attribute for cookies to either `'Lax'` or `'Strict'`. This attribute prevents cookies from being sent in cross-site requests unless explicitly allowed.

To set the `SameSite` attribute for cookies in Rails, you can configure it in your `config/application.rb` file:

```
# config/application.rb

config.action_dispatch.cookies_same_site_protection = :lax
```

This configuration ensures that cookies are sent with same-site requests by default.

By implementing these measures, you can significantly reduce the risk of CSRF attacks in your Ruby on Rails application. It's crucial to keep your application and gems up-to-date to benefit from the latest security enhancements and to regularly perform security assessments to identify and mitigate potential vulnerabilities.

Section 12.4: SQL Injection and Parameterization

SQL injection is a severe security vulnerability that can occur when user input is not properly sanitized before being included in SQL queries. Attackers can exploit this vulnerability to execute arbitrary SQL code, potentially leading to unauthorized access, data theft, or data manipulation. In this section, we'll discuss how to prevent SQL injection in your Ruby on Rails application through parameterization.

1. Active Record and Parameterization

Ruby on Rails encourages the use of the Active Record ORM (Object-Relational Mapping) for database interactions. Active Record automatically handles parameterization when querying the database, making SQL injection attacks highly unlikely.

Here's an example of a parameterized query using Active Record:

```
# Avoid this (not parameterized)
unsafe_query = "SELECT * FROM users WHERE username = '#{params[:username]}'"
results = ActiveRecord::Base.connection.execute(unsafe_query)

# Use this (parameterized)
safe_query = "SELECT * FROM users WHERE username = ?"
results = ActiveRecord::Base.connection.execute(safe_query, params[:username])
```

By using the ? placeholder in the query and providing user input as separate arguments, Active Record ensures that the input is properly escaped and prevents SQL injection.

2. Strong Parameters

When working with user input in Rails controllers, it's essential to use strong parameters to whitelist and sanitize the parameters that are allowed for mass assignment. This helps prevent unwanted parameters from being used in database operations.

```ruby
# In your controller
def create
  @user = User.new(user_params)
  # ...
end

private

def user_params
  params.require(:user).permit(:username, :email, :password)
end
```

In the user_params method, only the permitted attributes are allowed for mass assignment, providing an additional layer of protection against malicious input.

3. Sanitizing Input

In cases where you need to work with raw SQL or perform custom query construction, it's crucial to properly sanitize and validate user input before including it in SQL statements. Rails provides a set of methods for sanitizing input, such as sanitize_sql_array and sanitize_sql_for_conditions.

```ruby
# Using sanitize_sql_array
query = sanitize_sql_array(["SELECT * FROM users WHERE username = ?", params[:username]])

# Using sanitize_sql_for_conditions
query = sanitize_sql_for_conditions(["username = ?", params[:username]])
```

These methods ensure that user input is properly escaped and sanitized, reducing the risk of SQL injection.

4. Regular Security Audits

While parameterization and strong parameters can significantly mitigate SQL injection risks, it's essential to conduct regular security audits and testing, such as penetration testing and code reviews, to identify and address any potential vulnerabilities. Additionally, keeping your Rails application and gems up-to-date is crucial to benefit from security enhancements and patches.

By following these best practices and staying vigilant about security, you can reduce the likelihood of SQL injection vulnerabilities in your Ruby on Rails application, ensuring the safety of your data and users.

Section 12.5: Securing File Uploads and Authentication

File uploads and authentication are two crucial aspects of web applications. Ensuring their security is paramount to protect your application and user data. In this section, we'll discuss best practices for securing file uploads and authentication in your Ruby on Rails application.

1. Secure File Uploads

File uploads can be a security risk if not handled correctly. To secure file uploads in Rails, consider the following:

1.1. File Type Validation

Always validate the type of files being uploaded. You can use gems like `paperclip`, `CarrierWave`, or `Shrine` to handle file uploads and enforce content-type validation. Additionally, use server-side validation to double-check file types and prevent malicious uploads.

```ruby
# Using Paperclip gem for content-type validation
class User < ActiveRecord::Base
  has_attached_file :avatar
  validates_attachment_content_type :avatar, content_type: /\Aimage/
end
```

1.2. File Size Limit

Set a reasonable file size limit for uploads to prevent overloading your server or storage. You can configure this limit in your upload handler gem's settings.

```ruby
# Set maximum file size (in bytes) in Paperclip
class User < ActiveRecord::Base
  has_attached_file :avatar, :styles => { :medium => "300x300>", :thumb => "100x100>" }
  validates_attachment_size :avatar, less_than: 5.megabytes
end
```

1.3. Sanitize File Names

Ensure that file names are sanitized to prevent directory traversal attacks. Use a gem like `secure_headers` to help sanitize file names.

```ruby
# Using secure_headers gem for file name sanitization
config.action_dispatch.default_headers = {
  'X-Content-Type-Options' => 'nosniff',
  'X-Frame-Options' => 'SAMEORIGIN',
  'X-XSS-Protection' => '1; mode=block',
  'Content-Security-Policy' => "default-src 'self'",
  'X-Download-Options' => 'noopen',
  'X-Permitted-Cross-Domain-Policies' => 'none'
}
```

2. Authentication and Authorization

Authentication and authorization are essential for protecting sensitive areas of your application. Consider the following best practices:

2.1. Use Devise Gem

Devise is a widely-used gem for user authentication in Rails applications. It provides secure and customizable authentication features, including password hashing and user session management.

```
# Add Devise to your Gemfile
gem 'devise'
```

```
# Install Devise and generate configuration files
rails generate devise:install
rails generate devise User
```

2.2. Implement Role-Based Authorization

Use role-based authorization to control what users can access and modify. Gems like cancancan or Pundit can help you implement role-based authorization.

```
# Using Cancancan for role-based authorization
class Ability
  include CanCan::Ability

  def initialize(user)
    user ||= User.new

    if user.admin?
      can :manage, :all
    else
      can :read, :all
    end
  end
end
```

2.3. Store Passwords Securely

Ensure that user passwords are stored securely using salted and hashed password storage mechanisms. Devise handles this by default, but if you're implementing custom authentication, use gems like bcrypt for password hashing.

```
# Using bcrypt for password hashing
class User < ActiveRecord::Base
  has_secure_password
end
```

2.4. Protect Sensitive Routes

Use authentication filters to protect sensitive routes. For example, you can use `before_action` in your controllers to ensure that only authenticated users can access specific actions.

```ruby
class ApplicationController < ActionController::Base
  before_action :authenticate_user!
end
```

By following these best practices, you can strengthen the security of file uploads and user authentication in your Ruby on Rails application, reducing the risk of security vulnerabilities and data breaches. Security should always be a top priority in web development.

Chapter 13: Internationalization and Localization

In an increasingly globalized world, catering to a diverse audience is essential for web applications. Internationalization (i18n) and localization (l10n) are processes that allow your Ruby on Rails application to support multiple languages and regions. In this chapter, we will explore how to make your application multilingual, manage translation files, handle dynamic content localization, detect languages and regions, and work with time zones.

Section 13.1: Making Your App Multilingual

Making your Ruby on Rails application multilingual is the first step towards reaching a broader user base. Here are the key considerations for achieving multilingual support:

1. Set Up Internationalization (i18n)

Ruby on Rails provides built-in support for internationalization. To enable i18n, you need to configure your application to use the desired locale and translations. Start by modifying your config/application.rb file:

```
# config/application.rb
config.i18n.default_locale = :en
config.i18n.available_locales = [:en, :fr, :es]
```

In this example, we've set the default locale to English (:en) and made French (:fr) and Spanish (:es) available.

2. Translate Your Application

Next, you'll need to provide translations for different languages. Rails uses YAML files for translations. Create YAML files for each supported language under the config/locales directory. For instance, config/locales/en.yml, config/locales/fr.yml, and config/locales/es.yml.

```
# config/locales/en.yml
en:
  hello: Hello, World!
  welcome: Welcome to our app!
```

```
# config/locales/fr.yml
fr:
  hello: Bonjour, le Monde !
  welcome: Bienvenue sur notre application !
```

```
# config/locales/es.yml
es:
  hello: ¡Hola, Mundo!
  welcome: ¡Bienvenido a nuestra aplicación!
```

3. Use Translation Helpers

To display translated content in your views, use the t helper method followed by the translation key:

```
<!-- app/views/home/index.html.erb -->
<h1><%= t('hello') %></h1>
<p><%= t('welcome') %></p>
```

This will render the content based on the current locale. For instance, if the locale is set to :fr, the French translations will be displayed.

4. Dynamic Locale Switching

Allow users to switch the application's language dynamically. You can achieve this by setting the locale based on user preferences or the browser's language settings.

```
# app/controllers/application_controller.rb
before_action :set_locale

def set_locale
  I18n.locale = params[:locale] || I18n.default_locale
end
```

By following these steps, you can make your Ruby on Rails application multilingual, enhancing its accessibility to a broader audience. In the next sections, we'll delve into more advanced topics, such as working with translation files, dynamic content localization, language and region detection, and handling time zones.

Section 13.2: Working with Translation Files

In the previous section, we learned how to make our Ruby on Rails application multilingual. Now, let's explore how to work effectively with translation files and manage translations efficiently.

Organizing Translation Files

As your application grows, you'll have more translation keys and multiple languages to support. To keep your translation files organized, it's helpful to structure them hierarchically. Here's an example of how you can organize your translation files:

```
# config/locales/en.yml
en:
  welcome: Welcome to our app!
  navigation:
    home: Home
    about: About Us
    contact: Contact Us
  errors:
```

```yaml
    invalid_email: Invalid email address.
    required_field: This field is required.

# config/locales/fr.yml
fr:
  welcome: Bienvenue sur notre application !
  navigation:
    home: Accueil
    about: À Propos
    contact: Contactez-nous
  errors:
    invalid_email: Adresse email invalide.
    required_field: Ce champ est obligatoire.
```

By organizing your translations into namespaces like `navigation` and `errors`, you can easily locate and manage specific translations within your application.

Using Interpolations

Sometimes, you'll need to insert dynamic content into translated strings. You can achieve this using interpolation. Here's an example:

```yaml
# config/locales/en.yml
en:
  greeting: Hello, %{user_name}!
```

In your views or controllers, you can interpolate dynamic values like this:

```ruby
# In a controller or view
user_name = "John"
translated_greeting = I18n.t('greeting', user_name: user_name)
# Result: "Hello, John!"
```

Pluralization

Handling pluralization is another important aspect of translations. Different languages have different rules for plurals. Rails provides a way to handle pluralization easily:

```yaml
# config/locales/en.yml
en:
  apples:
    zero: No apples
    one: One apple
    other: %{count} apples
```

```yaml
# config/locales/fr.yml
fr:
  apples:
    zero: Pas de pommes
    one: Une pomme
    other: %{count} pommes
```

In your views or controllers, you can use the `pluralize` helper:

```
# In a controller or view
count = 5
translated_apples = I18n.t('apples', count: count)
# Result: "5 apples"
```

By following these practices, you can effectively manage your translation files and ensure that your application is ready for localization in multiple languages. In the next section, we'll explore dynamic content localization, which allows you to adapt your content based on the user's locale.

Section 13.3: Dynamic Content Localization

In this section, we'll dive into dynamic content localization, a feature that allows you to adapt your application's content based on the user's locale. This is especially useful when you need to display dates, times, and other locale-specific data.

Setting the Locale

In a Ruby on Rails application, you can set the locale for a user based on their preferences or location. Typically, you might detect the user's preferred language from their browser settings or allow them to manually select a language.

To set the locale for a user, you can use the `I18n` module's `locale` attribute. Here's how you can set the locale to English (assuming :en is defined in your translations):

```
# In a controller or a before action
I18n.locale = :en
```

You can change the locale to another supported language, such as :fr for French, to dynamically switch between languages based on user preferences.

Localizing Dates and Times

One common use case for dynamic content localization is displaying dates and times in a user's preferred format. Rails provides a simple way to do this using the l helper:

```
# In a view
date = Date.today
localized_date = l(date)
# Result (in English locale): "October 10, 2023"
```

This will format the date according to the locale's conventions.

Localizing Numbers

Similarly, you can localize numbers to use the correct decimal separator and digit grouping symbol for the user's locale:

```
# In a view
number = 1234.56
localized_number = number_to_currency(number)
# Result (in English locale): "$1,234.56"
```

Translating Dynamic Content

In some cases, you may have dynamic content that needs translation. You can achieve this using the `translate` helper:

```
# In a view
category = "Technology"
translated_category = translate(category)
# Result (in English locale): "Technology"
```

By using these localization techniques, you can create a more user-friendly and internationally accessible application that adapts to your users' preferences. In the next section, we'll explore language and region detection, which allows you to automatically set the user's locale based on their location or browser settings.

Section 13.4: Language and Region Detection

Language and region detection is a powerful feature for making your Ruby on Rails application even more user-friendly and accessible to a global audience. By automatically determining the user's preferred language or region, you can enhance their experience and ensure that content is displayed in a way that feels familiar to them.

Browser-Based Language Detection

One common way to detect a user's preferred language is by analyzing the `HTTP_ACCEPT_LANGUAGE` header sent by their browser. This header provides a list of languages and locales that the user's browser is set to prefer.

In Rails, you can access this information using the `request` object:

```
# In a controller or a before action
preferred_language = request.env['HTTP_ACCEPT_LANGUAGE']
```

You can then parse this header to determine the user's preferred language and adjust your application's behavior accordingly.

Using Geolocation for Region Detection

In addition to language detection, you might also want to detect the user's region or country. Geolocation can be used to determine the approximate location of the user based on their IP address.

There are Ruby gems and APIs available, such as Geocoder and IPinfo, that can help you perform geolocation-based region detection. Here's a basic example using the Geocoder gem:

```
# Gemfile
gem 'geocoder'

# In a controller or service
result = request.location
user_country = result.country
user_city = result.city
```

This information can be used to tailor content or features specific to a particular region.

Storing User Preferences

Once you've detected the user's preferred language or region, it's a good practice to store this information in the user's session or database profile. This allows you to remember their preferences for future visits.

For example, you can set the user's preferred language like this:

```
# In a controller or a before action
preferred_language = detect_user_language # Replace with your language detection logic
session[:user_language] = preferred_language
```

Then, you can use this stored preference to set the application's locale and deliver content in the user's chosen language.

Providing Language and Region Selection

It's essential to provide users with the option to manually select their preferred language or region. This ensures that users have control over their experience and can override automatic detection if needed. Implementing language and region selection typically involves creating a user settings page or a dropdown menu for users to choose their preferences.

By combining automatic detection with user-controlled preferences, you can create a flexible and inclusive Rails application that caters to a diverse user base with varying language and region requirements.

In the next section, we'll delve into handling time zones in Rails applications, which is crucial for displaying dates and times accurately to users across different regions.

Section 13.5: Handling Time Zones in Rails

Handling time zones in a Ruby on Rails application is essential for accurately displaying dates and times to users located in different parts of the world. Time zones ensure that timestamps are adjusted based on the user's geographical location, accounting for factors like daylight saving time.

Rails' Built-in Time Zone Support

Ruby on Rails provides robust built-in support for managing time zones. By default, Rails stores timestamps in the UTC (Coordinated Universal Time) format in the database, which is a best practice for consistent and unambiguous time representation. Rails then converts these timestamps to the user's selected time zone for display.

Setting the Default Time Zone

You can set the default time zone for your Rails application in the `config/application.rb` file:

```ruby
# config/application.rb
config.time_zone = 'Eastern Time (US & Canada)'
```

This setting ensures that all timestamps are converted and displayed in the specified time zone unless otherwise specified.

User-Specific Time Zones

To handle user-specific time zones, Rails typically relies on the user's preference, which can be stored in their user profile or session. When a user logs in or selects their time zone, you can set it as the current time zone for that session:

```ruby
# In a controller or a before action
user_time_zone = current_user.time_zone # Replace with your logic for fetching the user's preference
Time.zone = user_time_zone
```

From this point on, Rails will automatically adjust timestamps based on the user's selected time zone.

Displaying Time in Views

When displaying time in views, it's essential to use Rails' time zone-aware helpers to ensure that timestamps are presented correctly for the user's time zone. Common helpers include `time_ago_in_words` for displaying relative time and `l` for formatting time according to locale conventions.

```erb
# Display relative time
<%= time_ago_in_words(@article.created_at) %> ago
```

```erb
# Format time using user's time zone
<%= l(@event.start_time, format: :short) %>
```

The `l` helper allows you to specify the time format using localization files.

Daylight Saving Time

Rails also accounts for daylight saving time (DST) when converting timestamps. If a user is in a region that observes DST, Rails will adjust timestamps accordingly, ensuring that times are accurate throughout the year.

Time Zone Database Updates

It's important to keep your Rails application's time zone data up-to-date. Rails relies on the IANA Time Zone Database, and updates may be necessary to accommodate changes in time zone rules.

You can periodically update the time zone data by running:

```
rake time:zones:all
```

This ensures that your Rails application has the latest time zone information.

Handling time zones in your Rails application is crucial for providing a seamless and accurate user experience, especially for applications serving a global audience. With Rails' built-in support, you can easily manage time zones and display times correctly across various regions and time zones.

Chapter 14: Advanced Topics in Rails

Section 14.1: Background Jobs with Active Job

In a modern web application, tasks like sending emails, processing uploads, or performing computationally expensive operations can slow down the responsiveness of your application. To handle such tasks efficiently and keep your application responsive, Ruby on Rails provides a powerful solution called Active Job.

What is Active Job?

Active Job is a framework for declaring jobs and making them run on a variety of queuing backends. It provides a unified interface to work with different queuing systems such as Redis, Sidekiq, Delayed Job, Resque, and more. This abstraction allows you to write code that enqueues jobs in a consistent way, regardless of the queuing system you use.

Why Use Background Jobs?

Using background jobs with Active Job offers several benefits:

1. **Improved Responsiveness**: Long-running tasks can be offloaded to background jobs, ensuring that your application remains responsive to user requests.

2. **Scalability**: Background processing systems can scale independently from your web application, allowing you to handle increased workloads efficiently.

3. **Error Handling**: Most queuing systems offer mechanisms to handle failed jobs gracefully, including retries and error notification.

4. **Asynchronous Processing**: Jobs can be processed asynchronously, reducing the time users have to wait for resource-intensive operations to complete.

Getting Started with Active Job

To get started with Active Job, you'll need to:

1. **Generate a Job**: Use the `rails generate job` command to create a new job. For example:

   ```
   rails generate job SendWelcomeEmail
   ```

   This generates a job file in the `app/jobs` directory.

2. **Define the Job**: In the generated job file, define the work that should be performed when the job is executed. Here's an example:

   ```ruby
   class SendWelcomeEmailJob < ApplicationJob
     queue_as :default

     def perform(user)
       UserMailer.welcome_email(user).deliver_now
     end
   end
   ```

   In this example, the `perform` method defines the work to be done when the job is executed.

3. **Enqueue the Job**: To enqueue a job, you can call the `perform_later` method on an instance of the job class. For example:

   ```ruby
   SendWelcomeEmailJob.perform_later(current_user)
   ```

   This enqueues the job to be executed asynchronously.

4. **Run a Worker**: You'll need to have a worker process running to process the queued jobs. The setup depends on the queuing system you choose (e.g., Sidekiq, Delayed Job). You'll typically run a command like `rails jobs:work` to start a worker process.

Active Job provides a consistent and intuitive way to handle background tasks in your Rails application, making it easier to offload time-consuming operations and maintain a responsive user experience. It's a valuable tool for handling various asynchronous tasks efficiently and reliably.

Section 14.2: Building a Real-Time Chat Application

In this section, we will explore the development of a real-time chat application using Ruby on Rails. Real-time features are becoming increasingly important in modern web applications, allowing users to communicate instantly without the need to refresh the page. We will leverage Rails and a WebSocket library to achieve this functionality.

WebSocket and Rails

WebSocket is a protocol that enables full-duplex, bidirectional communication between a client (typically a web browser) and a server over a single, long-lived connection. This makes WebSocket ideal for real-time applications like chat.

To integrate WebSocket functionality into a Rails application, we can use a library like **Action Cable**, which is built into Rails since version 5.0. Action Cable provides the infrastructure for managing WebSocket connections and channels, making it easier to develop real-time features.

Getting Started

Here's an overview of the steps to build a real-time chat application in Rails:

1. **Generate a New Rails Application**: If you don't have an existing Rails application, create one using the `rails new` command.

2. **Generate a Chat Model**: Create a Chat model that will store chat messages in your database. You can use the `rails generate model` command for this.

3. **Set Up Action Cable**: Action Cable requires some configuration. Make sure it's enabled in your Rails application by adding it to your `config/application.rb` file:

   ```
   config.action_cable.mount_path = '/cable'
   ```

4. **Create a Chat Channel**: Generate an Action Cable channel for the chat:

   ```
   rails generate channel Chat
   ```

   This will create a `chat_channel.rb` file in the `app/channels` directory.

5. **Define Chat Logic**: In the `chat_channel.rb` file, you can define the logic for handling WebSocket connections and chat messages. For example, you can use the `stream_from` method to broadcast messages to subscribers.

6. **Create a Chat Interface**: On the front end, create a chat interface using JavaScript and HTML. You'll need to establish a WebSocket connection to the `/cable` endpoint and use JavaScript to handle incoming and outgoing messages.

7. **Broadcast Messages**: When a user sends a chat message, you can use Action Cable to broadcast that message to all connected clients in real time.

8. **Store Messages**: Store chat messages in your database so that users can see past messages when they join a chat room.

9. **Authentication and Authorization**: Implement authentication and authorization to ensure that users can only access and participate in the chat rooms they are allowed to.

10. **Testing**: Write tests to ensure the reliability and correctness of your chat application, especially the real-time features.

11. **Deployment**: Deploy your Rails application to a production server, ensuring that Action Cable is correctly configured.

Building a real-time chat application is a complex task that involves both backend and frontend development. However, with the power of Ruby on Rails and Action Cable, you can create a robust and interactive chat experience for your users.

The specifics of building a chat application can vary based on your requirements and design choices. This section provides a high-level overview, and you may need to delve deeper into Rails, JavaScript, and WebSocket technologies to implement the full functionality of your chat application.

Section 14.3: Implementing Single Sign-On (SSO)

Single Sign-On (SSO) is a mechanism that allows users to log in once and gain access to multiple applications without the need to log in separately for each one. In this section, we'll explore how to implement SSO in a Ruby on Rails application, enhancing user experience and security.

The Benefits of SSO

Implementing SSO in your Rails application offers several advantages:

1. **Streamlined User Experience**: Users can log in once and access multiple applications seamlessly. This reduces friction and improves user satisfaction.

2. **Enhanced Security**: SSO can improve security by enforcing strong authentication methods and centralized user access control. It reduces the risk of password-related vulnerabilities.

3. **Centralized User Management**: User accounts and permissions can be managed centrally, simplifying user provisioning and de-provisioning across multiple systems.

4. **Compliance and Auditing**: SSO can aid in compliance with regulations like GDPR and HIPAA, as access and authentication logs are centralized for auditing purposes.

To implement SSO in your Rails application, you can use industry-standard protocols like **OAuth2 or OpenID Connect (OIDC)**. These protocols allow your application to act as a Service Provider (SP) and integrate with an Identity Provider (IdP) for authentication.

Here are the basic steps to implement SSO in a Rails application:

1. **Choose an Identity Provider**: Select an Identity Provider that supports OAuth2 or OIDC. Popular choices include Okta, Auth0, Keycloak, and even social media platforms like Google, Facebook, or GitHub.

2. **Register Your Application**: Register your Rails application with the chosen Identity Provider. This typically involves providing details about your application, such as its name and callback URLs.

3. **Configure Your Rails Application**: In your Rails application, you'll need to configure an OAuth2 or OIDC gem (e.g., `omniauth-oauth2` or `omniauth-openid-connect`) to handle authentication requests and responses.

4. **Implement User Authentication**: Write code to handle the authentication flow. This includes handling callbacks from the IdP, validating tokens, and creating or updating user records in your application's database.

5. **Protect Routes**: Implement authorization checks to protect routes that require authentication. You can use libraries like `cancancan` or `Pundit` for fine-grained access control.

6. **Implement Logout**: Implement a logout mechanism that clears the user's session and logs them out of both your application and the IdP.

7. **Testing and Debugging**: Thoroughly test your SSO implementation, including different authentication scenarios and error handling. Debugging tools provided by your chosen IdP can be invaluable.

8. **User Provisioning**: Depending on your requirements, you may need to implement user provisioning and de-provisioning when a user logs in or out.

9. **Error Handling and Logging**: Implement robust error handling and logging to diagnose and resolve issues quickly.

10. **Documentation**: Document the SSO integration process for your team and future reference.

By following these steps, you can successfully implement SSO in your Rails application, providing a seamless and secure authentication experience for your users across multiple services and applications.

Remember that the specific implementation details may vary depending on your chosen Identity Provider and the gem you use for authentication. Always refer to the documentation provided by your IdP and the gem's documentation for the most accurate instructions.

Section 14.4: GraphQL with Ruby on Rails

GraphQL is a query language for your API and a server-side runtime for executing those queries by specifying the data you need from your API. In this section, we'll explore how to implement GraphQL in a Ruby on Rails application, enabling more efficient and flexible data retrieval.

Understanding GraphQL

GraphQL offers several advantages over traditional REST APIs:

1. **Efficient Data Fetching**: With GraphQL, clients can request exactly the data they need, avoiding over-fetching or under-fetching of data. This results in more efficient data transfers over the network.

2. **Single Endpoint**: GraphQL typically exposes a single endpoint for all data operations, reducing the number of network requests compared to REST APIs, which often require multiple endpoints for different resources.

3. **Strongly Typed**: GraphQL APIs are strongly typed, which means that clients receive predictable and well-documented responses. The GraphQL schema serves as a contract between the client and server.

4. **Batching Requests**: Clients can batch multiple requests into a single query, further reducing the number of round-trips to the server.

5. **Real-time Data**: GraphQL can be combined with subscriptions to enable real-time data updates, making it suitable for applications with dynamic content.

Implementing GraphQL in Rails

To implement GraphQL in your Ruby on Rails application, you'll typically use the `graphql-ruby` gem, which provides the necessary tools to define your GraphQL schema and execute queries.

Here are the basic steps to implement GraphQL in a Rails application:

1. **Install the Gem**: Add the `graphql` gem to your Rails project by adding it to your Gemfile and running `bundle install`.

2. **Define Your Schema**: Create a GraphQL schema that defines the types and queries your API will support. This schema typically resides in a file like `schema.graphql` or

`schema.rb`. Define custom types for your data and specify how clients can query and mutate that data.

3. **Implement Resolvers**: Resolvers are responsible for fetching data for specific fields in your schema. Implement resolver functions that fetch data from your database, external APIs, or other sources.

4. **Configure Your Route**: Configure a route in your Rails application to expose the GraphQL endpoint. This is often done in your `config/routes.rb` file.

5. **Authentication and Authorization**: Implement authentication and authorization mechanisms as needed for your GraphQL queries and mutations. You can use gems like `Devise` or `CanCanCan` for this purpose.

6. **Testing**: Write tests to ensure that your GraphQL schema and resolvers work as expected. Tools like `rspec-graphql` can assist in testing.

7. **Documentation**: Consider using tools like GraphQL's built-in documentation or third-party solutions like GraphQL-Ruby's `graphql-docs` gem to provide documentation for your API.

8. **Batching and N+1 Query Protection**: Implement batching of database queries to avoid N+1 query problems, which can occur in GraphQL when fetching related data for multiple records.

9. **Real-time Updates**: If you want to enable real-time updates, you can integrate subscriptions using libraries like `graphql-subscriptions`.

10. **Error Handling**: Implement robust error handling to provide meaningful error messages to clients.

Once you've followed these steps, your Ruby on Rails application will have a fully functional GraphQL API, allowing clients to query, mutate, and subscribe to data in a flexible and efficient manner.

Remember to refer to the `graphql-ruby` documentation and guides for detailed instructions and best practices when implementing GraphQL in your Rails application.

Section 14.5: Exploring Microservices Architecture

Microservices architecture is a software design approach that structures an application as a collection of small, independent, and loosely coupled services. Each microservice is responsible for a specific piece of functionality, and they communicate with each other through well-defined APIs. In this section, we'll explore microservices architecture in the context of Ruby on Rails applications.

Microservices have gained popularity due to their potential benefits, including:

1. **Scalability**: Microservices allow you to scale individual components of your application independently, making it easier to handle increased load on specific services.

2. **Flexibility**: Each microservice can be developed, deployed, and maintained independently. This flexibility enables teams to choose the most suitable technology stack for each service.

3. **Continuous Delivery**: Smaller codebases and independent deployments streamline the continuous integration and continuous delivery (CI/CD) pipeline.

4. **Resilience**: Isolating services means that a failure in one microservice doesn't necessarily affect the entire application. It's easier to implement fault tolerance and graceful degradation.

5. **Team Autonomy**: Different teams can work on separate microservices, fostering autonomy and faster development cycles.

Implementing Microservices in Ruby on Rails

To implement a microservices architecture in a Ruby on Rails application, you'll typically follow these guidelines:

1. **Service Decoupling**: Identify the different functionalities or domains within your application that can be separated into individual microservices. Each microservice should have a well-defined scope.

2. **API Communication**: Microservices communicate with each other through APIs. Consider using RESTful APIs or GraphQL for this purpose. Ensure that your APIs are well-documented and versioned to maintain compatibility.

3. **Data Isolation**: Microservices should have their databases or data stores. This prevents data coupling between services and allows each service to use the most appropriate database technology.

4. **Authentication and Authorization**: Implement authentication and authorization mechanisms for your microservices. You may use technologies like JWT (JSON Web Tokens) or OAuth for secure communication.

5. **Service Discovery**: Implement service discovery and load balancing to facilitate communication between services, especially in dynamic environments where instances of microservices can scale up or down.

6. **Monitoring and Logging**: Set up comprehensive monitoring and logging for each microservice to gain insights into their performance, health, and error handling.

7. **Error Handling**: Implement a robust error handling strategy that allows microservices to gracefully handle failures and return meaningful error responses.

8. **Testing**: Write tests for each microservice to ensure that they function correctly in isolation and when integrated with other services.

9. **Deployment and Orchestration**: Use containerization technologies like Docker and orchestration tools like Kubernetes to manage the deployment and scaling of microservices.

10. **Documentation**: Maintain documentation for each microservice's API, including endpoints, data models, and usage examples.

11. **Cross-Cutting Concerns**: Consider how to handle cross-cutting concerns such as logging, security, and monitoring consistently across all microservices.

12. **Observability**: Implement observability solutions like tracing and metrics collection to gain insights into the interactions between microservices.

13. **Scaling Strategies**: Define strategies for scaling individual microservices based on their specific requirements.

Microservices architecture is a powerful way to build scalable and maintainable applications, but it also introduces complexities in terms of orchestration, communication, and data consistency. Careful planning and adherence to best practices are essential for successful microservices implementations.

In conclusion, microservices offer the flexibility to build complex systems while maintaining agility and scalability. However, it's crucial to carefully design, implement, and manage microservices to realize their full benefits in your Ruby on Rails applications.

Chapter 15: Version Control and Collaboration

Section 15.1: Git Essentials for Rails Developers

Version control is a fundamental tool for developers, and Git is one of the most widely used version control systems. In this section, we'll explore the essential concepts of Git and how it applies to Rails development.

What is Git?

Git is a distributed version control system that allows multiple developers to work on the same project simultaneously while keeping track of changes, history, and collaboration seamlessly. It was created by Linus Torvalds in 2005 and has since become the de facto standard for version control in the software development industry.

Key Git Concepts

Repository (Repo)

A Git repository, often referred to as a "repo," is a directory that contains all the files and metadata necessary for version control. It stores the entire history of a project, including changes made over time.

Commit

A commit is a snapshot of your code at a specific point in time. It represents a set of changes you've made to your project. Each commit has a unique identifier called a "SHA-1 hash."

Branch

A branch is a parallel line of development in Git. It allows developers to work on features or bug fixes independently without affecting the main codebase. Common branches include "master" for the main codebase and feature branches for specific tasks.

Merge

Merging is the process of combining changes from one branch into another. It's often used to incorporate new features or bug fixes developed in separate branches back into the main codebase.

Pull Request (PR)

A pull request is a mechanism for submitting code changes to a project's main branch. It allows other developers to review and discuss the proposed changes before they are merged.

Clone

Cloning is the process of creating a copy of a Git repository on your local machine. It allows you to work on the project locally and push changes back to the remote repository when you're ready.

Using Git in Rails Development

Git plays a crucial role in Rails development, facilitating collaboration among team members and tracking changes in your application. Here are some common Git commands and practices used in Rails development:

Initializing a Git Repository

To start using Git in your Rails project, navigate to the project's root directory and run:

```
git init
```

This initializes a new Git repository in the project folder.

Adding Files to the Staging Area

Before committing changes, you need to add files to the staging area. Use the following command to stage one or more files:

```
git add filename
```

Committing Changes

Once you've staged your changes, commit them with a descriptive message:

```
git commit -m "Your commit message here"
```

Creating and Switching Branches

To create a new branch and switch to it, use:

```
git checkout -b new-branch-name
```

Pushing Changes

When you're ready to share your changes with others or update the remote repository, use:

```
git push origin branch-name
```

Pulling Changes

To retrieve changes made by others from the remote repository, use:

```
git pull origin branch-name
```

Resolving Merge Conflicts

Sometimes, when merging branches, conflicts may arise if two or more developers have modified the same part of a file. You'll need to manually resolve these conflicts by editing the affected files.

Git Hosting Services

To collaborate effectively, teams often use Git hosting services like GitHub, GitLab, or Bitbucket. These platforms provide features such as code review, issue tracking, and project management integrated with Git repositories.

In Rails development, using Git and a hosting service can greatly streamline teamwork and code management. It ensures that changes are tracked, reviewed, and integrated smoothly into the project.

Understanding Git fundamentals is crucial for Rails developers, as it empowers efficient collaboration, code management, and version control in the Rails ecosystem. Whether you're working on a solo project or as part of a team, Git is an invaluable tool in your Rails development toolkit.

Section 15.2: Collaborating with Git and GitHub

Collaboration is at the heart of software development, and Git, combined with platforms like GitHub, plays a pivotal role in enabling effective collaboration among developers. In this section, we'll explore how to collaborate with Git and GitHub in the context of Rails development.

Forking a Repository

When collaborating on an open-source project or contributing to a shared codebase, it's common to start by forking the original repository. Forking creates a copy of the repository under your GitHub account, allowing you to make changes without affecting the original project.

To fork a repository on GitHub, follow these steps:

1. Visit the repository you want to fork on GitHub.

2. Click the "Fork" button in the upper-right corner of the repository page.

3. Choose your GitHub account as the destination for the fork.

Cloning a Forked Repository

Once you've forked a repository, you can clone it to your local machine to start working on it. Use the following command to clone your forked repository:

```
git clone https://github.com/your-username/repo-name.git
```

Replace `your-username` with your GitHub username and `repo-name` with the name of the repository.

Adding a Remote

To keep your forked repository in sync with the original repository, you can add a remote that points to the original repository. This is helpful when you want to pull in changes made by others.

```
git remote add upstream https://github.com/original-owner/repo-name.git
```

Replace `original-owner` with the username of the owner of the original repository and `repo-name` with the name of the repository.

Making Changes and Committing

Now that you have a local copy of the forked repository, you can make changes to the code. After making changes, stage and commit them using Git as you normally would.

```
git add .
git commit -m "Your commit message here"
```

Pushing Changes to Your Fork

To update your fork on GitHub with the changes you've made locally, push the commits to your forked repository.

```
git push origin branch-name
```

Replace `branch-name` with the name of the branch you're working on.

Creating a Pull Request

Once you've pushed your changes to your forked repository on GitHub, you can create a pull request (PR) to propose your changes to the original repository. A PR serves as a way to discuss and review the changes with the project maintainers.

1. Visit your forked repository on GitHub.

2. Click the "New Pull Request" button.

3. Select the branch containing your changes in the "base" dropdown. This is typically the "master" branch of the original repository.

4. Select the branch you've been working on in the "compare" dropdown.

5. Add a title and description to your pull request, explaining the changes and why they should be merged.

6. Click the "Create Pull Request" button.

Reviewing and Merging Pull Requests

On the original repository, project maintainers or collaborators will review your pull request. They may provide feedback, request changes, or approve and merge your changes.

GitHub provides tools for discussing and reviewing code within pull requests, making it easier to collaborate effectively.

Keeping Your Fork in Sync

To keep your fork up to date with the original repository, you'll need to regularly fetch and merge changes from the original repository's "master" branch into your fork. Here are the steps:

1. Fetch changes from the original repository:

    ```
    git fetch upstream
    ```

2. Switch to your local "master" branch:

    ```
    git checkout master
    ```

3. Merge changes from the original repository's "master" branch into your local "master" branch:

    ```
    git merge upstream/master
    ```

4. Push the updated "master" branch to your fork on GitHub:

    ```
    git push origin master
    ```

This process ensures that your fork remains synchronized with the latest changes in the original repository.

Collaborating with Git and GitHub is a fundamental skill for Rails developers, enabling them to contribute to open-source projects, work effectively in teams, and manage code changes efficiently. By following these practices, you can participate in collaborative Rails development projects with confidence.

Section 15.3: Managing Feature Branches

In collaborative Rails development, managing feature branches is essential for organized and efficient teamwork. Feature branches allow developers to work on specific features or fixes without interfering with the main development branch, usually "master" or "main." This section discusses the best practices for creating, managing, and collaborating on feature branches in a Rails project.

Creating a Feature Branch

1. **Start from the Main Branch**: Before creating a feature branch, ensure you are on the main development branch (e.g., "master" or "main"). Use the following command to switch to the main branch:

    ```
    git checkout master
    ```

2. **Create a New Branch**: To create a new feature branch, use the following command:

    ```
    git checkout -b feature/my-new-feature
    ```

    Replace feature/my-new-feature with a descriptive name for your feature. Prefixing it with "feature/" is a common convention.

3. **Push the New Branch**: If you want to collaborate with others on this feature, push the branch to your remote repository (usually on GitHub):

    ```
    git push origin feature/my-new-feature
    ```

Working on the Feature

Once the feature branch is created, you can start working on your feature or bug fix. Make regular commits to save your progress:

```
git add .
git commit -m "Implement feature XYZ"
```

Collaborative Development

Collaboration often involves multiple developers working on the same feature. To ensure a smooth collaboration process, follow these practices:

1. **Pull Latest Changes**: Regularly pull the latest changes from the main branch into your feature branch to stay up to date:

    ```
    git checkout feature/my-new-feature
    git pull origin master
    ```

2. **Push and Share**: When you have completed a part of the feature or fixed an issue, push your branch to the remote repository:

    ```
    git push origin feature/my-new-feature
    ```

    Share your progress by creating a pull request (PR) for discussion and code review.

3. **Review and Discuss**: Collaborators can review your code within the PR. Use GitHub's review tools to leave comments, suggest changes, or approve the PR.

4. **Continuous Integration**: Ensure that your feature branch passes automated tests and continuous integration (CI) checks. Many Rails projects use tools like Travis CI or GitHub Actions for CI.

Once your feature is complete and has received necessary approvals, it's time to merge it into the main branch. Here's how:

1. **Update Your Feature Branch**: Before merging, ensure your feature branch is up to date with the latest changes from the main branch:

```
git checkout feature/my-new-feature
git pull origin master
```

2. **Rebase (Optional)**: Consider rebasing your feature branch to incorporate the latest changes gracefully. This can result in a cleaner commit history:

```
git rebase master
```

3. **Create a Pull Request**: On GitHub, create a pull request from your feature branch to the main branch.

4. **Review and Merge**: Collaborators review the pull request, and when approved, it can be merged.

5. **Delete Feature Branch**: After merging, delete the feature branch both locally and on the remote repository:

```
git branch -d feature/my-new-feature    # Delete locally
git push origin --delete feature/my-new-feature    # Delete remotely
```

Summary

Managing feature branches is crucial for organized and efficient Rails development collaboration. By following these best practices, Rails developers can work seamlessly on specific features or bug fixes while maintaining a clean and maintainable codebase. Collaborative development in Rails projects is greatly facilitated by feature branches and code review processes.

Section 15.4: Code Reviews and Best Practices

Code reviews are a crucial part of maintaining code quality and ensuring that the Rails project continues to evolve smoothly. In this section, we'll explore the importance of code reviews and some best practices for conducting them effectively in a Rails development environment.

Why Code Reviews Matter

Code reviews serve several essential purposes:

1. **Quality Assurance**: Code reviews help catch and rectify errors, bugs, and logical issues in the code before they make it into the production environment.

2. **Knowledge Sharing**: They provide an opportunity for team members to learn from each other. Junior developers can benefit from the expertise of senior developers through feedback and suggestions.

3. **Maintainability**: Code reviews ensure that code adheres to established coding standards and follows best practices, making it easier to maintain and extend in the future.

4. **Consistency**: They help maintain code consistency across the project, ensuring that all team members follow the same coding conventions.

Best Practices for Code Reviews

Here are some best practices to follow when conducting code reviews in a Rails project:

1. **Use a Code Review Tool**: Leverage code review tools like GitHub Pull Requests or GitLab Merge Requests, which provide a structured environment for code review discussions and comments.

2. **Focus on Small Changes**: Review smaller, more manageable changes. This makes it easier to spot issues and provide meaningful feedback.

3. **Review the Right Files**: Ensure that the review covers the essential files, such as code changes, tests, and documentation.

4. **Understand the Context**: Reviewers should understand the context of the changes, including the problem being solved and the proposed solution. Ask questions if necessary.

5. **Follow Coding Standards**: Ensure that the code adheres to coding standards and style guides established for the project.

6. **Check for Code Smells**: Look for code smells or anti-patterns that might indicate potential issues or areas for improvement.

7. **Test Coverage**: Ensure that new code is adequately covered by tests, and verify that the tests pass.

8. **Security Considerations**: Pay attention to potential security vulnerabilities, such as SQL injection or cross-site scripting (XSS) issues.

9. **Avoid Personal Criticism**: Keep feedback constructive and avoid personal criticism. Focus on the code and its quality.

10. **Review Iteratively**: Consider reviewing code iteratively, with multiple reviewers providing feedback in different areas. This can help catch different types of issues.

11. **Documentation**: Ensure that code changes are documented appropriately, including any updates to README files or inline code comments.

12. **Consistency**: Check for consistency not only in code style but also in naming conventions, error handling, and approach.

13. **Performance**: If applicable, review for potential performance bottlenecks or inefficiencies.

Code Review Workflow

Typically, a code review workflow in a Rails project involves the following steps:

1. The developer creates a pull request (PR) with their changes.

2. Team members or reviewers are assigned to review the PR.

3. Reviewers go through the code, leave comments, and discuss any issues or improvements.

4. The developer addresses the feedback, makes necessary changes, and pushes the updates to the PR.

5. Reviewers reevaluate the changes, and the process continues iteratively until the code is approved.

6. Once approved, the code is merged into the main branch and becomes part of the project.

Conclusion

Code reviews are a fundamental aspect of Rails development, promoting code quality, collaboration, and continuous improvement. By following best practices and maintaining a constructive and open-minded approach to code reviews, Rails teams can ensure that their projects remain robust and maintainable throughout their lifecycle.

Section 15.5: Resolving Merge Conflicts

Merge conflicts can be an inevitable part of collaborative software development, especially when multiple developers are working on the same codebase simultaneously. In this section, we'll explore what merge conflicts are, why they occur, and how to resolve them effectively within a Rails project.

Understanding Merge Conflicts

A merge conflict happens when two or more branches of code, typically within Git, have diverged, and Git cannot automatically reconcile the differences. This occurs when:

- Developer A makes changes to a file, commits those changes, and pushes them to a shared repository.
- Simultaneously, Developer B makes changes to the same file, commits those changes, and pushes them to the same shared repository.
- When Developer B attempts to merge their changes into the main branch or another shared branch, Git detects conflicting changes in the same file and cannot determine which version to keep.

Why Merge Conflicts Occur

Merge conflicts can occur for various reasons, including:

1. **Parallel Development**: When multiple developers work on the same file concurrently, there's a higher chance of conflicts.

2. **Divergent Changes**: If two developers modify the same lines of code differently, Git cannot automatically decide which change to accept.

3. **Branch Merges**: Conflicts may arise when merging feature branches into the main development branch.

4. **Rebasing**: When developers rebase their branches onto another branch, conflicts may occur if the rebased changes conflict with existing ones.

Resolving Merge Conflicts

Here are steps to effectively resolve merge conflicts within a Rails project:

1. **Detect the Conflict**: Git will indicate which files have conflicts. These files will contain conflict markers, such as <<<<<<<, =======, and >>>>>>>, indicating the conflicting sections.

2. **Open the Conflicted File**: Open the conflicted file in a text editor or integrated development environment (IDE).

3. **Manually Resolve Conflicts**: Examine the conflicting sections and decide which changes to keep or modify. Delete the conflict markers (<<<<<<<, =======, and >>>>>>>) and make the necessary adjustments.

```
def some_method
<<<<<<< HEAD
  # Code from the current branch
  ...
=======
  # Code from the incoming branch
  ...
>>>>>>> incoming-branch
end
```

4. **Save the File**: After manually resolving conflicts, save the file.

5. **Commit the Changes**: Stage the resolved file by adding it to the commit, and then commit the changes. Include a meaningful commit message indicating that you've resolved the merge conflict.

6. **Push the Changes**: Once conflicts are resolved and committed, push the changes to the remote repository.

7. **Verify the Merge**: If you were merging branches, verify that the merge was successful and that the code now works as expected.

Conflict Resolution Tools

Many integrated development environments (IDEs) and Git clients offer built-in tools for resolving conflicts graphically, making the process more straightforward. These tools often allow you to choose which changes to keep, discard, or manually edit.

Conflict Prevention

To reduce the likelihood of merge conflicts in a Rails project, consider the following best practices:

- Communicate with team members to avoid working on the same sections of code simultaneously.
- Break down larger tasks into smaller, focused branches to minimize overlap.
- Regularly update your local repository with changes from the remote repository to keep your branch up-to-date.
- Use feature flags or toggles to isolate and hide in-progress features until they are ready for integration.

By understanding and effectively resolving merge conflicts, Rails developers can maintain a smooth and collaborative development process while ensuring code integrity and stability.

Chapter 16: Continuous Learning and Resources

In the fast-paced world of Ruby on Rails development, continuous learning is not just beneficial—it's essential. Staying up-to-date with the latest trends, tools, and best practices is crucial for career growth and building robust Rails applications. This chapter explores various strategies and resources for continuous learning within the Rails ecosystem.

Section 16.1: Staying Up-to-Date with Rails

Ruby on Rails is a dynamic framework that continually evolves. Staying current with the latest updates, gems, and techniques is vital for any Rails developer. Here's how you can stay up-to-date:

1. Official Rails Documentation

The official Ruby on Rails documentation is an invaluable resource. It provides comprehensive information about the framework's features, changes in each release, and guides for various topics. Regularly check for updates and refer to the documentation when exploring new Rails features or solving problems.

2. Rails Release Notes

Stay informed about new Rails releases by reading their release notes. These notes highlight new features, improvements, and changes introduced in each version. Understanding what's new can help you leverage the latest capabilities in your projects.

3. Rails Mailing List and Forums

Join the Rails community by participating in the official mailing list and forums. These platforms are where developers discuss problems, share solutions, and exchange knowledge. Subscribing to the mailing list can keep you informed about ongoing discussions and important announcements.

4. Blogs and Newsletters

Follow Rails-related blogs and newsletters. Many experienced developers share their insights, best practices, and tutorials through blogs. Subscribe to newsletters that curate relevant articles and updates. Some popular Rails-related blogs include Ruby on Rails Guides, ThoughtBot, and GoRails.

5. Podcasts and Webinars

Rails-related podcasts and webinars can be an enjoyable way to learn about industry trends and hear from experienced developers. Listen to podcasts during your commute or downtime to stay updated on the latest news and insights.

6. Social Media and GitHub

Follow Rails core team members and active contributors on social media platforms like Twitter. GitHub is another excellent resource for tracking changes in Rails repositories and exploring the source code. GitHub's "Watch" feature can notify you of repository updates.

7. Online Courses and Books

Consider enrolling in online courses that cover advanced Rails topics or specific areas like testing, security, or performance optimization. Additionally, explore books written by Rails experts that delve into in-depth topics.

8. Conferences and Meetups

Attend Rails-related conferences and meetups in your area or virtually. These events offer opportunities to network, learn from experts, and gain insights into emerging trends.

9. Online Communities

Participate in online communities, such as Ruby on Rails subreddits or Stack Overflow. You can ask questions, share your knowledge, and learn from others' experiences.

10. Open Source Contributions

Contributing to open source Rails projects is an excellent way to deepen your understanding of the framework. It allows you to work alongside experienced developers and make a positive impact on the Rails community.

11. Experiment and Build

Hands-on experience is one of the most effective ways to learn. Create personal projects or contribute to open source projects. Experiment with new gems, libraries, and techniques to expand your skill set.

Remember that learning is an ongoing process, and it's essential to allocate time for continuous improvement. Embrace new challenges, stay curious, and remain engaged with the Rails community to enhance your skills and career in Ruby on Rails development.

Section 16.2: Joining the Rails Community

One of the most rewarding aspects of being a Ruby on Rails developer is the sense of community and collaboration that permeates the ecosystem. Joining the Rails community can provide numerous benefits, including learning opportunities, networking, and a sense of belonging. In this section, we'll explore how to become an active part of the Rails community.

1. Attend Local Meetups

Rails enthusiasts often organize local meetups where developers can gather, share knowledge, and discuss projects. These meetups provide a great opportunity to meet fellow developers in your area, learn from one another, and stay updated on local developments.

2. Engage on Online Platforms

Participating in online communities is another way to connect with Rails developers worldwide. Platforms like GitHub, Reddit, and Stack Overflow have dedicated Rails sections where you can ask questions, share insights, and help others with their Rails-related challenges.

3. Contribute to Open Source

Contributing to open source Rails projects is not only a way to give back to the community but also a fantastic learning experience. You can start by exploring Rails-related repositories on GitHub and looking for issues labeled as "good first issue" or "beginner-friendly." Contributing code, fixing bugs, or improving documentation are all valuable contributions.

4. Attend Rails Conferences

Rails conferences, whether in-person or virtual, bring together Rails developers from around the world. These events feature talks, workshops, and networking opportunities. Consider attending conferences like RailsConf to immerse yourself in the Rails community and learn from industry experts.

5. Join the Rails Core Team

For experienced developers looking to make a significant impact, becoming part of the Rails core team is a prestigious goal. This requires a deep understanding of the framework, consistent contributions, and recognition from existing core team members. It's a challenging but rewarding path for those dedicated to advancing Rails.

6. Engage on Social Media

Follow Rails developers, maintainers, and organizations on social media platforms like Twitter and LinkedIn. Engage in discussions, share interesting content, and stay informed about community updates and events.

7. Organize Your Own Events

If there's no local Rails meetup in your area, consider starting one yourself. Organizing events or webinars on specific Rails topics can help you connect with other developers and establish yourself as a leader in your community.

8. Collaborate on Projects

Collaboration is at the heart of the Rails community. Consider partnering with other developers on projects, whether they are personal, open source, or commercial. Working together not only enhances your skills but also fosters strong connections within the community.

9. Write Blog Posts and Documentation

Sharing your knowledge through blog posts, tutorials, or documentation contributions is a valuable way to give back to the Rails community. Your insights and experiences can help other developers overcome challenges and learn new techniques.

10. Be Supportive and Inclusive

Lastly, remember to be supportive and inclusive in your interactions with fellow Rails developers. Encourage newcomers, offer help when needed, and promote a positive and welcoming atmosphere within the community.

Becoming an active member of the Rails community can enrich your career, expand your knowledge, and introduce you to like-minded developers who share your passion for Ruby on Rails. Whether you're a beginner or an experienced developer, there's a place for everyone in the vibrant Rails community.

Section 16.3: Recommended Blogs and Podcasts

In the ever-evolving world of Ruby on Rails, staying up-to-date with the latest trends, best practices, and industry insights is essential. One way to achieve this is by following blogs and podcasts dedicated to Rails development. These resources offer a wealth of knowledge, news, and discussions that can help you sharpen your skills and stay informed about the latest developments. In this section, we'll explore some recommended Rails-related blogs and podcasts.

Blogs

1. **Ruby on Rails Official Blog**: The official blog of Ruby on Rails is a primary source for announcements, updates, and insights from the Rails core team. It provides in-depth information about new releases and features.

2. **The Pragmatic Studio Blog**: The Pragmatic Studio offers Rails-focused courses, and their blog covers various Rails-related topics, including tutorials and best practices.

3. **GoRails Blog**: GoRails is a popular online learning platform for Rails developers. Their blog features tutorials, tips, and articles on various aspects of Rails development.

4. **Hashrocket Blog**: Hashrocket is a development consultancy with a strong focus on Rails. Their blog covers advanced topics, case studies, and best practices.

5. **BigBinary Blog**: BigBinary is known for its contributions to the Rails ecosystem. Their blog provides detailed insights into Rails updates, tutorials, and engineering practices.

6. **DockYard Blog**: DockYard specializes in custom software, and their blog includes articles about Rails development, design, and UX.

7. **RubyFlow**: RubyFlow is a community-driven platform where developers share their favorite articles and resources related to Ruby and Rails. It's an excellent place to discover new content.

Podcasts

1. **The Ruby on Rails Podcast**: Hosted by Brittany Martin, this podcast features interviews with prominent figures in the Rails community. It covers topics like new features, best practices, and the experiences of Rails developers.

2. **Remote Ruby**: A podcast hosted by three experienced Ruby and Rails developers, Remote Ruby explores various Ruby-related topics, including Rails, web development, and programming in general.

3. **Ruby Rogues**: While not Rails-specific, the Ruby Rogues podcast discusses Ruby and related technologies. It often features discussions on Rails best practices and development strategies.

4. **Code with Jason**: Jason Swett hosts this podcast, where he shares insights and interviews other developers about Ruby on Rails, testing, and software engineering.

5. **The Ruby Blend**: A podcast that covers Ruby, Rails, and other web development topics. It's a great source of information and discussions relevant to Rails developers.

These blogs and podcasts offer a treasure trove of information, tutorials, and insights that can help you enhance your Ruby on Rails skills. Whether you're a beginner or an experienced developer, regularly following these resources can keep you informed, inspired, and engaged with the Rails community.

Section 16.4: Books and Online Courses

Books and online courses are valuable resources for anyone looking to deepen their knowledge of Ruby on Rails. They provide structured learning paths, comprehensive coverage of topics, and the opportunity to learn from experienced authors and instructors. In this section, we'll explore some recommended books and online courses that can help you advance your Rails development skills.

Books

1. **"Agile Web Development with Rails" by Sam Ruby, David B. Copeland, and Dave Thomas**: This classic book is a go-to resource for Rails beginners. It walks you through building a complete web application and covers key Rails concepts.

2. **"Rails Tutorial" by Michael Hartl**: Also known as the "Rails Tutorial Book," this resource is widely regarded for its step-by-step approach to building a Rails application. It includes extensive coverage of testing and deployment.

3. **"The Pragmatic Programmer's Guide to Ruby" by Dave Thomas and Andy Hunt**: While not Rails-specific, this book is an excellent resource for mastering Ruby, the language behind Rails. A strong Ruby foundation is crucial for Rails development.

4. **"Design Patterns in Ruby" by Russ Olsen**: Understanding design patterns is important for writing clean and maintainable Rails code. This book explores design patterns in the context of Ruby, making it a valuable read for Rails developers.

5. **"Metaprogramming Ruby" by Paolo Perrotta**: Metaprogramming is a powerful technique in Ruby, and this book delves into the art of writing code that writes code. It's a must-read for Rails developers who want to leverage the full potential of Ruby.

Online Courses

1. Ruby on Rails Tutorial by Michael Hartl: This online course complements the book mentioned earlier. It offers video lectures, exercises, and hands-on coding experience to help you become proficient in Rails.

2. Udemy - The Complete Ruby on Rails Developer Course: This course covers a wide range of Rails topics, including building real-world applications, testing, and deploying to production.

3. Coursera - Ruby on Rails Web Development Specialization: Offered by Johns Hopkins University, this specialization consists of several courses that take you from the basics of Ruby to building web applications with Rails.

4. Pluralsight - Ruby on Rails: The Big Picture: This course provides an overview of Ruby on Rails, making it a good starting point for those new to the framework.

5. Codecademy - Learn Ruby on Rails: Codecademy offers an interactive and beginner-friendly introduction to Ruby on Rails. It's a great way to get hands-on experience.

These books and online courses cater to a wide range of skill levels, from beginners to experienced developers looking to deepen their expertise. Depending on your learning style and goals, you can choose the resources that best suit your needs and accelerate your journey to becoming a proficient Rails developer.

Section 16.5: Contributing to Open Source Rails Projects

Contributing to open source Rails projects is an excellent way to enhance your skills, give back to the community, and collaborate with experienced developers from around the world. In this section, we'll explore how you can get involved in open source Rails projects and make meaningful contributions.

Why Contribute to Open Source?

Contributing to open source has several benefits:

1. **Skill Development**: You'll gain hands-on experience and improve your coding skills by working on real-world projects.

2. **Networking**: You can connect with developers, maintainers, and enthusiasts who share your interests and passion for Rails.

3. **Resume Enhancement**: Open source contributions look impressive on your resume and can make you more appealing to potential employers.

4. **Giving Back**: It's a way to give back to the Rails community and support the tools and libraries you rely on.

How to Contribute

1. Choose a Project:

- **GitHub**: Start by exploring Rails-related projects on GitHub. You can filter projects by language (Ruby) and topic (Rails).

2. Read Documentation:

- **ReadMe**: Carefully read the project's README file. It provides essential information on how to contribute, code of conduct, and project goals.

3. Pick an Issue:

- **Issues**: Most projects have a list of issues that need attention. Look for "good first issue" or "beginner-friendly" labels if you're new to contributing.

4. Fork the Repository:

- **Fork**: Fork the project's repository on GitHub. This creates a copy of the project under your GitHub account.

5. Clone the Repository:

- **Clone**: Use `git clone` to create a local copy of the repository on your computer.

```
git clone https://github.com/your-username/project-name.git
```

6. Create a Branch:

- **Branch**: Create a new branch for your contribution. It's best practice to name the branch based on the issue you're addressing.

```
git checkout -b issue-fix
```

7. Make Changes:

- **Code**: Write your code to address the issue you selected. Follow the project's coding standards and conventions.

8. Test Your Changes:

- **Tests**: Run existing tests and write new ones to ensure your changes don't introduce regressions.

```
bundle exec rake test
```

9. Commit and Push:

- **Commit**: Commit your changes and push them to your forked repository.

```
git commit -m "Fix issue #123"
git push origin issue-fix
```

10. Create a Pull Request:

- **PR**: Visit the original project on GitHub and create a pull request (PR) from your branch. Provide a clear description of your changes.

11. Collaborate:

- **Feedback**: Be prepared for feedback from project maintainers and other contributors. Collaboration is key to improving your code.

12. Stay Engaged:

- **Communication**: Stay engaged with the project's community, join discussions, and continue contributing.

Finding Open Source Rails Projects

Here are some popular open source Rails projects to get you started:

- Ruby on Rails: The official Rails repository.
- Spree Commerce: An open-source e-commerce solution.
- Discourse: A modern forum software built with Rails.
- Forem: An open-source discussion platform.
- Solidus: A customizable e-commerce platform.

Remember, contributing to open source is about learning, collaborating, and making a positive impact on projects you care about. Start small, be patient, and enjoy the journey of becoming an active open source contributor in the Rails community. Your contributions can help shape the future of Rails and benefit developers worldwide.

Chapter 17: Building and Launching Your Portfolio

Section 17.1: Creating a Portfolio Website

A portfolio website is a crucial tool for showcasing your skills, projects, and accomplishments as a Rails developer. It serves as an online resume and a place for potential employers or clients to learn more about you. In this section, we'll discuss how to create a compelling portfolio website using Ruby on Rails.

Why Do You Need a Portfolio Website?

1. **Professional Image**: A well-designed portfolio website demonstrates professionalism and commitment to your craft.

2. **Showcase Your Work**: It's a platform to display your projects, code samples, and case studies to potential employers or clients.

3. **Personal Branding**: Establish your personal brand as a Rails developer and make a memorable impression.

4. **Career Advancement**: A strong online presence can open up new job opportunities and freelance projects.

Steps to Create a Portfolio Website

1. Planning

- **Objective**: Define the purpose of your portfolio. What do you want to showcase? Your projects, skills, or blog posts?

- **Target Audience**: Identify who your portfolio is for. Is it potential employers, clients, or the Rails community?

- **Content**: Plan the content you want to include, such as project descriptions, your bio, and contact information.

2. Design

- **Theme**: Choose a clean and professional design that reflects your style. Consider using Bootstrap or other CSS frameworks.

- **Layout**: Decide on the layout of your homepage, project pages, and contact page.

- **Typography and Colors**: Select fonts and colors that align with your personal brand.

3. Development

- **Rails Project**: Create a new Rails project to build your portfolio.

- **Routes and Views**: Define routes and views for your homepage, project pages, and other sections.

- **Models**: If you plan to include a blog, create a model for blog posts.

- **Styling**: Apply CSS styles to achieve the desired design.

4. Content

- **Projects**: Create pages for each project you want to showcase. Include project descriptions, screenshots, and links to the code.

- **About Me**: Write a compelling bio that highlights your skills and experiences.

- **Contact Information**: Provide a way for visitors to get in touch with you, such as a contact form or email address.

- **Blog (Optional)**: If you plan to write blog posts, create and publish your first articles.

5. Testing

- **Testing**: Test your website on different browsers and devices to ensure responsiveness and functionality.

6. Deployment

- **Hosting**: Choose a hosting provider. Heroku is a popular choice for Rails projects.

- **Domain**: Register a domain name that reflects your name or brand.

- **Deployment**: Deploy your Rails application to your chosen hosting platform.

7. Maintenance

- **Regular Updates**: Keep your portfolio updated with new projects and blog posts.

- **Monitoring**: Monitor your website's performance and security.

Example Code (Routes and Views)

Here's a simplified example of how you can define routes and views for your portfolio website in Rails:

```ruby
# config/routes.rb
Rails.application.routes.draw do
  root 'home#index'
  get '/projects', to: 'projects#index'
  get '/projects/:id', to: 'projects#show', as: 'project'
  get '/about', to: 'home#about'
  get '/contact', to: 'home#contact'
  # Add routes for blog if needed
end
```

```erb
<!-- app/views/home/index.html.erb -->
<h1>Welcome to My Portfolio</h1>
<!-- Add your homepage content here -->
```

```erb
<!-- app/views/projects/index.html.erb -->
<h2>Projects</h2>
<!-- List your projects here with descriptions and links -->

<!-- app/views/projects/show.html.erb -->
<h2><%= @project.title %></h2>
<!-- Display details of a specific project -->

<!-- app/views/home/about.html.erb -->
<h2>About Me</h2>
<!-- Write your bio here -->

<!-- app/views/home/contact.html.erb -->
<h2>Contact Me</h2>
<!-- Provide contact information or a contact form -->
```

Creating your portfolio website is an exciting endeavor that can help you stand out in the Rails community and advance your career. Keep it updated with your latest projects and experiences to showcase your growth as a Rails developer.

Section 17.2: Showcasing Your Projects

Once you've set up your portfolio website, the next step is to effectively showcase your projects. Your projects are the heart of your portfolio, and how you present them can make a significant difference in how potential employers or clients perceive your skills and expertise. In this section, we'll explore strategies for showcasing your projects on your portfolio website.

Organizing Your Projects

1. **Categorization**: Consider grouping your projects into categories. For example, you could have separate sections for web applications, mobile apps, open-source contributions, or personal projects.

2. **Featured Projects**: Highlight a few key projects on your homepage to grab visitors' attention. These should be your most impressive or relevant projects.

3. **Project Descriptions**: Write clear and concise descriptions for each project. Explain the problem you solved, the technologies used, and the impact of the project.

4. **Screenshots and Demos**: Include screenshots or video demos of your projects. Visual elements can make your projects more engaging.

Providing Context

5. **Tech Stack**: Mention the technologies and programming languages you used in each project. This gives visitors a sense of your skills.

6. **Challenges**: Describe any challenges you faced during the project and how you overcame them. This demonstrates problem-solving abilities.

7. **Teamwork**: If you worked on a project as part of a team, mention your role and contributions. Collaboration skills are valuable.

Code Samples

8. **GitHub Links**: Provide links to the GitHub repositories of your projects. This allows visitors to explore your code and contributions.

9. **Code Snippets**: Include code snippets or highlight specific parts of your code that showcase your programming skills. Explain the significance of the code.

Results and Impact

10. **Results**: Share the outcomes of your projects. Did your project lead to increased user engagement, revenue, or efficiency?

11. **User Feedback**: If available, include user testimonials or feedback. This adds credibility to your work.

Continuous Improvement

12. **Updates**: Mention any updates or improvements you've made to the project since its initial launch. It shows your commitment to ongoing learning.

Example Portfolio Project Entry

Here's an example of how you can structure a project entry on your portfolio website:

Project Title: E-Commerce Website

Description: Developed a fully functional e-commerce website using Ruby on Rails. Implemented features such as user authentication, product search, shopping cart, and secure payment processing. The website saw a 30% increase in sales within the first quarter of launch.

Tech Stack: Ruby on Rails, PostgreSQL, Bootstrap, Devise (authentication), Stripe (payment processing)

Challenges: Overcoming the challenge of securely handling payments and integrating Stripe for payment processing. Implemented background jobs for order processing to improve website performance.

GitHub Repository: GitHub Link

Screenshots: Include screenshots or links to view the live website.

By effectively showcasing your projects, you provide visitors with a clear understanding of your skills, experience, and the value you can bring to their projects or organizations. Keep your project entries concise, informative, and visually appealing to make a lasting impression.

Section 17.3: Writing a Developer Blog

Maintaining a developer blog as part of your portfolio website can be a powerful tool for showcasing your expertise, sharing your knowledge, and building your personal brand. In this section, we'll explore the benefits of having a developer blog and offer tips on how to create engaging and valuable blog content.

The Benefits of a Developer Blog

1. **Demonstrating Expertise**: Writing about technical topics demonstrates your knowledge and expertise in your field. It can help establish you as a thought leader.

2. **Building an Online Presence**: A blog can significantly contribute to your online presence. It allows you to connect with a broader audience, including potential employers, clients, and other developers.

3. **Portfolio Expansion**: Each blog post is like a mini-portfolio item. It showcases your ability to explain complex topics and solve problems.

4. **Learning and Sharing**: Writing about what you've learned is a powerful way to solidify your own understanding of a topic. It also contributes to the knowledge base of the developer community.

Tips for Writing Engaging Blog Posts

5. **Choose Relevant Topics**: Select topics that are relevant to your target audience and align with your expertise. Consider what challenges your readers might face and how your knowledge can help them.

6. **Clear and Structured Content**: Write in a clear and structured manner. Use headings, subheadings, and bullet points to make your content easy to read.

7. **Visual Elements**: Incorporate visual elements like images, diagrams, and code snippets to illustrate your points.

8. **Practical Examples**: Provide practical examples and code samples when discussing technical topics. These can help readers understand and implement your insights.

9. **Engage with Readers**: Encourage reader engagement by inviting comments, questions, and discussions. Respond promptly to comments to foster a sense of community.

10. **Consistency**: Establish a regular posting schedule. Consistency helps build a loyal readership.

11. **Promote Your Blog**: Share your blog posts on social media, developer forums, and relevant communities to increase visibility.

12. **Tutorials**: Create step-by-step tutorials on how to accomplish specific tasks or solve common problems in your field.

13. **Case Studies**: Share real-world case studies or project breakdowns, highlighting your problem-solving skills.

14. **Best Practices**: Offer insights into best practices, coding standards, and optimization techniques.

15. **Challenges and Solutions**: Describe challenges you've encountered in your projects and how you overcame them.

16. **Technology Reviews**: Write reviews and comparisons of tools, libraries, or frameworks you've used.

17. **Career Insights**: Share your experiences, career advice, and tips for professional development.

Example Blog Post Structure

Here's a basic structure you can follow for your developer blog posts:

Title: Choose a descriptive and engaging title.

Introduction: Provide an overview of what the post will cover and why it's relevant.

Body: Break down the topic into sections with clear headings. Include explanations, examples, and code snippets as needed.

Conclusion: Summarize the main points and offer any concluding thoughts or recommendations.

Call to Action: Encourage readers to comment, share, or explore related posts on your blog.

By maintaining a developer blog that provides value to your target audience, you can effectively showcase your expertise, connect with peers, and contribute to the developer community. Over time, your blog can become a valuable asset in your portfolio, highlighting your growth as a developer and thought leader.

Section 17.4: Networking and Job Hunting Tips

Networking is an essential aspect of advancing your career as a developer. Whether you're actively job hunting or simply looking to expand your professional connections, effective networking can open doors to new opportunities and foster personal growth. In this section, we'll explore some networking and job hunting tips tailored for developers.

1. **Attend Tech Meetups and Conferences**: Participating in local meetups, conferences, and tech events is an excellent way to meet like-minded professionals. These events often feature presentations, workshops, and networking sessions.

2. **Online Communities**: Engage in online communities such as GitHub, Stack Overflow, Reddit, and tech-specific forums. Share your knowledge, ask questions, and offer assistance to others.

3. **LinkedIn**: Optimize your LinkedIn profile to showcase your skills and achievements. Connect with fellow developers, colleagues, and recruiters. Join relevant LinkedIn groups and participate in discussions.

4. **Open Source Contributions**: Contribute to open source projects related to your interests or field. Collaborating with others on GitHub or similar platforms can help you establish a reputation within the developer community.

5. **Personal Website and Blog**: Maintain a personal website or blog to showcase your portfolio, share your expertise, and demonstrate your passion for development.

Job Hunting Tips
6. **Online Job Platforms**: Utilize job search platforms like LinkedIn Jobs, Indeed, Glassdoor, and specialized tech job boards to find job openings tailored to your skills and interests.

7. **Customize Your Resume**: Tailor your resume to highlight relevant skills and experiences for each job application. Use keywords from the job description to improve your chances of getting noticed by applicant tracking systems (ATS).

8. **Build a Portfolio**: Create an online portfolio showcasing your projects, code samples, and accomplishments. Include links to your GitHub repositories and personal website.

9. **Practice Technical Interviews**: Prepare for technical interviews by practicing coding challenges, data structure questions, and behavioral interview questions. Websites like LeetCode and HackerRank offer valuable resources for practice.

10. **Networking for Job Opportunities**: Leverage your professional network to inquire about job openings and referrals. Employee referrals can increase your chances of getting an interview.

11. **Stay Informed**: Stay up-to-date with industry trends, technologies, and company news. This knowledge can be valuable during interviews and networking conversations.

Effective Networking Etiquette
12. **Be Genuine**: Approach networking with a genuine interest in building meaningful relationships, rather than solely seeking job opportunities.

13. **Follow Up**: After networking events or informational interviews, send a personalized thank-you email expressing your appreciation and willingness to stay connected.

14. **Offer Value**: Seek opportunities to help others, whether it's providing assistance with a coding problem or sharing valuable resources.

15. **Professionalism**: Maintain professionalism in all your interactions, both online and offline. Treat every interaction as a chance to make a positive impression.

16. **Leverage Your Alumni Network**: Connect with alumni from your educational institution who may be working in the tech industry. Alumni networks often have valuable resources and connections.

Networking and job hunting require patience and persistence. Building meaningful relationships and finding the right job opportunity can take time, but the effort you invest in networking and your job search can pay off in the form of career advancement and personal growth. Remember that networking is a two-way street, and the relationships you cultivate can benefit both you and your connections in the long run.

Section 17.5: Preparing for Job Interviews

Preparing for job interviews is a crucial step in landing your dream role as a developer. Interviews can be challenging, but with the right preparation, you can increase your chances of success. In this section, we'll cover some essential tips and strategies to help you excel in technical interviews and non-technical aspects of job interviews.

Technical Interview Preparation

1. **Review Data Structures and Algorithms**: Brush up on fundamental data structures like arrays, linked lists, trees, and hash tables. Understand common algorithms, searching, sorting, and graph algorithms.

2. **Coding Challenges**: Practice coding challenges on platforms like LeetCode, HackerRank, and CodeSignal. Solve problems related to the programming languages and technologies you'll be using in your target job.

3. **Whiteboard and Online Coding**: If your interview involves whiteboard coding or coding on a shared online platform, practice this style of coding. Focus on explaining your thought process clearly.

4. **Project Portfolio**: Be ready to discuss your past projects in detail. Explain the challenges you faced, your problem-solving approach, and the technologies you used. Prepare to showcase your code and discuss design decisions.

5. **Behavioral Questions**: Prepare answers to common behavioral questions using the STAR method (Situation, Task, Action, Result). Be ready to share examples of your teamwork, problem-solving, and conflict resolution skills.

6. **Company Research**: Research the company thoroughly. Understand its mission, values, products or services, and recent news. This knowledge will help you tailor your responses to show your alignment with the company culture.

7. **Common Interview Questions**: Practice answering common non-technical questions such as "Tell me about yourself," "Why do you want to work here?" and "What are your strengths and weaknesses?"

8. **Questions for the Interviewer**: Prepare thoughtful questions to ask the interviewer. Questions about the team, company culture, and expectations demonstrate your interest and engagement.

9. **Dress Code**: Determine the company's dress code and choose appropriate attire for the interview. When in doubt, it's generally better to be slightly overdressed than underdressed.

10. **Portfolio Presentation**: If you have a portfolio, be ready to present it. Walk the interviewer through your projects, explaining the problem, your role, the technologies used, and the outcomes.

11. **Soft Skills**: Practice good communication skills, active listening, and maintaining eye contact. Confidence, enthusiasm, and a positive attitude are also key.

Mock Interviews and Feedback

12. **Mock Interviews**: Conduct mock interviews with a friend or mentor, or use online platforms that offer mock interview services. Simulating real interview scenarios can help you build confidence.

13. **Feedback**: After mock interviews or real interviews, seek feedback. Constructive criticism can help you identify areas for improvement and refine your interview skills.

Logistics and Practicalities

14. **Technical Setup**: Ensure your technical setup, including your computer, camera, microphone, and internet connection, is reliable. Test everything well before the interview.

15. **Interview Schedule**: Confirm the interview schedule, including the date, time, and format (in-person, phone, video). Plan to arrive early for in-person interviews or log in early for virtual interviews.

16. **Documentation**: Prepare all necessary documents such as your resume, cover letter, ID, and any certifications. Have them organized and easily accessible.

17. **Follow-Up**: Send a thank-you email after the interview, expressing your gratitude for the opportunity and reiterating your interest in the position.

Remember that interview preparation is an ongoing process. It's not just about cramming information but building your skills and confidence over time. Approach interviews with a growth mindset, where each interview, whether successful or not, is a learning opportunity that brings you closer to your career goals.

By following these interview preparation tips, you'll be well-equipped to tackle technical and non-technical aspects of job interviews and present yourself as a strong candidate to potential employers.

Chapter 18: Case Studies and Real-World Projects

Section 18.1: Case Study 1: Building an E-commerce Platform

In this section, we'll delve into a comprehensive case study on building an e-commerce platform using Ruby on Rails. E-commerce platforms are complex applications that involve various components, including product catalog management, user authentication, shopping cart functionality, order processing, and payment integration. This case study will provide you with insights into the architecture, features, and best practices for developing a robust e-commerce platform.

Understanding the Requirements

Before diving into development, it's crucial to gather and understand the project requirements. In the case of an e-commerce platform, some common requirements may include:

- User registration and authentication.
- Product catalog with categories and search functionality.
- Shopping cart management.
- Checkout process with multiple payment options.
- Order tracking and history.
- Admin panel for product and order management.
- Security measures to protect user data and transactions.
- Scalability to handle high traffic during peak times.
- Responsive design for a seamless mobile shopping experience.

Database Design

The foundation of any e-commerce platform is a well-designed database schema. You'll need tables to store information about users, products, orders, payments, and more. Consider using Ruby on Rails' Active Record migrations to define and manage your database schema.

Implementing User Authentication

User authentication is a fundamental component. You can leverage the Devise gem or roll your custom authentication solution using Bcrypt for password hashing. Ensure secure password storage and implement features like email confirmation and password reset.

Building the Product Catalog

Create models and controllers for managing products and categories. Implement features like product image uploads, product reviews, and product recommendations based on user behavior.

Shopping Cart and Checkout

Develop a shopping cart system that allows users to add and remove items. Implement a seamless checkout process with various payment options, such as credit card payments and third-party payment gateways like PayPal.

Order Processing

Design a system for order processing, including order confirmation emails, order history, and the ability for users to track their orders.

Admin Panel

Build an admin panel to manage products, categories, and orders. Admins should have the ability to edit product details, view and process orders, and manage user accounts.

Security Measures

Implement security best practices to protect user data and transactions. Use HTTPS for secure communication, employ Cross-Site Request Forgery (CSRF) protection, and sanitize user inputs to prevent SQL injection and Cross-Site Scripting (XSS) attacks.

Scalability

Consider using a cloud-based infrastructure that can automatically scale to handle increased traffic during peak shopping seasons. Optimize database queries and use caching to improve performance.

Testing and Quality Assurance

Thoroughly test your e-commerce platform with unit tests, integration tests, and user acceptance testing. Ensure that payment processing is secure and that the platform works flawlessly across different devices and browsers.

Launch and Maintenance

Once your e-commerce platform is ready, plan for a successful launch. Monitor the platform for performance issues and security vulnerabilities regularly. Keep the software and libraries updated to address security patches and feature enhancements.

This case study provides an overview of the steps involved in building an e-commerce platform with Ruby on Rails. Keep in mind that each e-commerce project may have unique requirements and challenges, so adapt and extend these guidelines as needed to meet your specific goals. Building an e-commerce platform is a significant undertaking, but with careful planning and execution, you can create a successful online shopping experience for your users.

Section 18.2: Case Study 2: Creating a Social Networking App

In this section, we'll explore a case study focused on creating a social networking application using Ruby on Rails. Social networking apps, like Facebook or Twitter, involve complex features for user profiles, posts, comments, likes, and social interactions. This case study will guide you through the process of architecting and implementing such a platform.

Understanding the Requirements

Before diving into development, it's crucial to gather and understand the project requirements. For a social networking app, the requirements may include:

- User registration and authentication.
- User profiles with avatars and personal information.
- The ability to create and publish posts.
- Social interactions, such as following and being followed by other users.
- Commenting on posts.
- Liking posts and comments.
- Notifications for user interactions.
- Messaging between users.
- Content moderation and reporting functionality.
- Responsive design for mobile and desktop.

Database Design

The heart of a social networking app lies in its database schema. You'll need tables to store information about users, posts, comments, likes, follows, messages, and more. Consider using Ruby on Rails' Active Record migrations for defining and managing your database schema.

Implementing User Authentication

User authentication is fundamental. You can use popular gems like Devise or roll out your custom solution. Ensure secure password storage, user session management, and features like email confirmation and password reset.

User Profiles and Avatars

Create models and controllers for user profiles. Users should be able to upload avatars and provide personal information like a bio. Consider using gems like CarrierWave for avatar uploads.

Post Creation and Feeds

Implement the ability for users to create posts and view a feed of posts from users they follow. Use Rails associations to link users to their posts and the posts to users.

Social Interactions

Design the ability for users to follow other users, like posts, and comment on posts. Implement features like real-time notifications for interactions.

Messaging System

Build a messaging system that allows users to send private messages to each other. You can implement real-time messaging using technologies like WebSockets with ActionCable.

Content Moderation

Implement content moderation features to filter out inappropriate content. Allow users to report content that violates community guidelines.

Responsive Design

Ensure that your social networking app is responsive and provides a seamless experience on both mobile and desktop devices. Utilize CSS frameworks like Bootstrap to simplify styling.

Testing and Quality Assurance

Comprehensively test your social networking app, including unit tests, integration tests, and user acceptance testing. Pay special attention to features like messaging and notifications to ensure they work reliably.

Launch and Maintenance

Plan a successful launch for your social networking app and continuously monitor its performance and security. Keep the software and libraries up-to-date to address security vulnerabilities and add new features as needed.

Creating a social networking app with Ruby on Rails is a substantial endeavor, but with careful planning and diligent development, you can create a platform that connects users and fosters social interactions. Remember that user engagement and community building are key aspects of a successful social networking app, so focus on delivering a compelling user experience.

Section 18.3: Case Study 3: Developing a SaaS Application

In this section, we'll dive into a case study focused on developing a Software as a Service (SaaS) application using Ruby on Rails. SaaS applications are web-based software solutions that are hosted in the cloud and delivered to users over the internet. They often serve multiple customers and provide various subscription plans.

Concept and Planning

Before starting development, it's crucial to define the concept and purpose of your SaaS application. Consider factors like target audience, unique selling points, and monetization strategies. Conduct market research to identify your potential competitors and understand the needs of your target users.

Multi-Tenancy Architecture

A core aspect of SaaS applications is their ability to serve multiple tenants (customers) while keeping their data isolated. Implement a multi-tenancy architecture, where each tenant has its separate database schema or shared tables with a tenant identifier. The `acts_as_tenant` gem can help with this.

User Authentication and Roles

Implement user authentication with different roles (e.g., admin, user, and premium user). Use gems like Devise and CanCanCan for user management and authorization.

Subscription Billing

For SaaS applications, managing subscriptions and billing is critical. Integrate with payment gateways like Stripe or Braintree to handle subscription plans, billing cycles, and payment processing. The `stripe-rails` gem can simplify Stripe integration.

User Onboarding

Create a smooth onboarding process for new users. Guide them through account setup and introduce them to key features. Consider using a wizard-like interface to collect essential information.

Feature Development

Prioritize feature development based on user needs and feedback. Use Agile development methodologies like Scrum or Kanban to manage your development workflow efficiently.

Data Analytics and Insights

Implement data analytics and reporting features to provide users with insights into their usage of the SaaS application. Tools like Google Analytics or custom analytics dashboards can be valuable.

Scalability and Performance

Design your SaaS application for scalability from the beginning. Use tools like Redis for caching and background job processing. Employ content delivery networks (CDNs) for asset delivery and optimize database queries.

Security and Compliance

Security is paramount in SaaS applications. Protect user data with encryption, implement proper access controls, and regularly conduct security audits. Ensure compliance with data protection regulations like GDPR or HIPAA if applicable.

Testing and Quality Assurance

Thoroughly test your SaaS application, including unit tests, integration tests, and user acceptance testing. Test different subscription scenarios, payment failures, and user roles to ensure robust functionality.

Documentation and Support

Provide comprehensive documentation for your SaaS application, including user guides, API documentation, and troubleshooting guides. Set up support channels, such as email or chat, to assist users with inquiries and issues.

Continuous Deployment and Monitoring

Implement a continuous integration and continuous deployment (CI/CD) pipeline to automate testing and deployment processes. Monitor the application's performance, uptime, and error rates using tools like New Relic or Sentry.

User Feedback and Iteration

Collect user feedback actively and use it to drive improvements and new feature development. Iterate on your SaaS application based on user input to enhance user satisfaction and retention.

Developing a SaaS application with Ruby on Rails offers the advantage of rapid development and a rich ecosystem of gems and libraries. However, building a successful SaaS product requires careful planning, robust architecture, and ongoing commitment to user experience and support.

Section 18.4: Case Study 4: Building a Content Management System

In this section, we'll explore the development of a Content Management System (CMS) using Ruby on Rails. A CMS is a web application that enables users to create, manage, and publish digital content such as articles, blog posts, images, and videos. It's a versatile platform commonly used for websites, blogs, and online publications.

Planning and Requirements

Before diving into development, it's crucial to define the requirements of your CMS. Identify the types of content your system will manage, user roles (e.g., editors, authors, and administrators), and the desired features such as content scheduling, tagging, and revision history.

Data Modeling

Design the database schema to represent various content types, categories, tags, and users. Use Rails migrations to create tables for these entities and establish associations between them.

```ruby
# Example migration for creating an articles table
class CreateArticles < ActiveRecord::Migration[6.0]
  def change
    create_table :articles do |t|
      t.string :title
      t.text :content
      t.references :user, foreign_key: true
      t.timestamps
    end
  end
end
```

Authentication and Authorization

Implement user authentication and authorization to control access to the CMS. Devise is a popular gem for user management, while CanCanCan can handle role-based authorization.

```ruby
# Using Devise for user authentication
class User < ApplicationRecord
  devise :database_authenticatable, :registerable,
         :recoverable, :rememberable, :validatable
end
```

Content Creation and Editing

Create a user-friendly interface for content creation and editing. Use rich text editors like Trix or Froala for text formatting and media embedding. Implement version control or content revision history to track changes.

Categories and Tags

Allow content categorization through categories and tagging. Use gems like ActsAsTaggableOn for tag management and establish associations between content and categories.

```ruby
# Example model associations for tagging
class Article < ApplicationRecord
  acts_as_taggable
end
```

Content Publishing and Scheduling

Implement content publishing and scheduling capabilities. Define publication dates and statuses (e.g., draft, published) for content items. Use background job processing with gems like Sidekiq for scheduling publication.

SEO and URL Handling

Optimize your CMS for search engines by generating SEO-friendly URLs, implementing meta tags, and enabling XML sitemaps. The FriendlyId gem can simplify URL handling.

```ruby
# Using FriendlyId for SEO-friendly URLs
class Article < ApplicationRecord
  extend FriendlyId
  friendly_id :title, use: :slugged
end
```

Media Management

Allow users to upload and manage media files such as images and videos. Use storage solutions like Amazon S3 or Cloudinary for efficient media storage and retrieval.

User-Friendly Interface

Design an intuitive and responsive user interface (UI) for your CMS. Ensure that users can easily navigate, search, and manage their content.

Security and Access Control

Prioritize security by validating user inputs, protecting against cross-site scripting (XSS) and SQL injection attacks, and using secure authentication practices.

Scalability and Performance

Plan for scalability by optimizing database queries, caching frequently accessed content, and leveraging CDNs for media delivery. Implement background job processing for resource-intensive tasks.

Testing and Quality Assurance

Thoroughly test your CMS, including content creation, editing, and publishing workflows. Automate testing using frameworks like RSpec and Capybara.

Documentation and User Support

Provide comprehensive documentation for content creators and administrators. Offer user support channels for addressing inquiries and issues promptly.

Building a CMS with Ruby on Rails offers flexibility and extensibility, making it suitable for a wide range of content-driven websites and applications. Proper planning, user-focused design, and robust development practices are key to creating a successful CMS that meets the needs of both content creators and consumers.

Section 18.5: Lessons Learned from Real-World Projects

In this concluding section, we'll reflect on some valuable lessons learned from real-world Ruby on Rails projects. These insights can help you navigate common challenges and make informed decisions when working on your own projects.

1. Planning and Requirements Gathering

- **Lesson:** Thoroughly define project requirements, objectives, and user stories before development begins. Incomplete or unclear requirements can lead to scope creep and project delays.

2. Choosing the Right Gems

- **Lesson:** While gems can significantly speed up development, be selective. Avoid excessive gem dependencies to maintain project stability and prevent conflicts.

3. Database Optimization

- **Lesson:** Regularly optimize database queries and indexes. Improper database design or inefficient queries can lead to performance bottlenecks.

4. Testing and Test Coverage

- **Lesson:** Invest time in comprehensive testing. High test coverage and robust test suites catch bugs early and ensure the stability of your application.

5. Continuous Integration

- **Lesson:** Implement continuous integration (CI) early in your project. CI tools like Travis CI automate testing and ensure code quality with each commit.

6. Code Review

- **Lesson:** Conduct code reviews with your team. Code reviews lead to better code quality, knowledge sharing, and identification of potential issues.

7. Security Best Practices

- **Lesson:** Prioritize security from the beginning. Protect against common threats like XSS, CSRF, and SQL injection. Regularly update gems and dependencies for security patches.

8. Scalability

- **Lesson:** Design your application with scalability in mind. Plan for horizontal scaling, caching, and load balancing to handle increased traffic.

9. Documentation and Knowledge Sharing

- **Lesson:** Maintain comprehensive documentation. Share knowledge within your team and consider creating developer guides for onboarding new members.

10. User Experience (UX) and Feedback
- **Lesson:** Continuously gather user feedback and iterate on your application's user experience. User-centric design leads to higher satisfaction.

11. Version Control and Collaboration
- **Lesson:** Use version control effectively, and establish clear branching and merging workflows. Collaboration tools like Git and GitHub are essential for teamwork.

12. Error Monitoring and Logging
- **Lesson:** Implement error monitoring and logging solutions. Services like Rollbar or Sentry help you identify and fix issues proactively.

13. Performance Profiling
- **Lesson:** Profile your application's performance using tools like New Relic or Rack Mini Profiler. Identify bottlenecks and optimize accordingly.

14. Backup and Disaster Recovery
- **Lesson:** Regularly backup your data and have a disaster recovery plan in place. Data loss can be catastrophic without proper precautions.

15. Feedback Loops and Retrospectives
- **Lesson:** Conduct regular retrospectives to evaluate project progress and identify areas for improvement. Feedback loops foster continuous learning.

16. Community and Resources
- **Lesson:** Engage with the Ruby on Rails community. Online forums, meetups, and conferences offer networking opportunities and a wealth of knowledge.

17. Adaptability and Flexibility
- **Lesson:** Be adaptable to changing requirements and technologies. The tech landscape evolves, and flexibility is key to staying relevant.

18. Project Management and Communication
- **Lesson:** Effective project management and clear communication are crucial for successful project delivery. Tools like Slack and Trello can facilitate communication and task tracking.

19. Taking Breaks and Avoiding Burnout
- **Lesson:** Remember to take breaks and prioritize work-life balance. Burnout can hinder productivity and creativity.

20. Celebrating Successes
- **Lesson:** Celebrate project milestones and successes with your team. Recognizing achievements boosts morale and motivation.

By incorporating these lessons into your Ruby on Rails projects, you can increase your chances of success and create applications that are robust, maintainable, and user-friendly. Continuously learning and adapting is key to thriving in the ever-evolving field of web development.

Chapter 19: Future Trends in Rails Development

In this chapter, we'll explore emerging trends and technologies in the Ruby on Rails ecosystem and the wider web development landscape. Staying informed about these trends can help you make informed decisions, adopt best practices, and keep your Rails applications up to date.

Section 19.1: The Evolution of Ruby on Rails

Ruby on Rails has evolved significantly since its inception. While the core principles of Rails remain intact, several notable trends have shaped its development and usage over the years.

1. API-First Development

- **Trend:** Rails has embraced API-first development, making it easier to build robust APIs alongside traditional web applications. This trend aligns with the demand for mobile and single-page applications (SPAs).

2. JavaScript Integration

- **Trend:** Rails now integrates seamlessly with modern JavaScript frameworks and libraries. Technologies like Webpacker and the advent of JavaScript-driven front-end frameworks have become part of Rails projects.

3. Performance Optimization

- **Trend:** Rails continues to focus on performance improvements. Features like Action Cable (for real-time applications) and enhancements in database performance have been introduced.

4. Microservices and Modularization

- **Trend:** Microservices architecture has gained popularity. Rails developers increasingly build smaller, modular applications that communicate via APIs, allowing for scalability and maintainability.

5. Containerization and Docker

- **Trend:** Containerization, particularly with Docker, has become a standard for deploying Rails applications. It simplifies application deployment, scaling, and management.

6. Serverless Computing

- **Trend:** Serverless computing platforms like AWS Lambda have been integrated with Rails applications. This enables event-driven, cost-effective execution of code.

7. WebAssembly (Wasm)

- **Trend:** WebAssembly is gaining traction in Rails development. It allows running compiled code in the browser, opening up possibilities for high-performance web applications.

8. Progressive Web Apps (PWAs)

- **Trend:** Rails developers are exploring PWAs, which offer an app-like experience in web browsers. Rails provides tools for building offline-capable PWAs.

9. AI and Machine Learning

- **Trend:** Integrating AI and machine learning into Rails applications is becoming more accessible. Libraries like TensorFlow and services like AWS SageMaker are being used for ML tasks.

10. Community Contributions

- **Trend:** The Rails community remains vibrant. Contributions from developers worldwide continue to enhance the framework's features, security, and performance.

As you navigate the evolving Rails landscape, keep these trends in mind to make informed decisions about your projects. Embracing change and staying up-to-date can help you build modern, efficient, and competitive web applications. Remember that Rails' adaptability and commitment to developer productivity are constants amid these trends.

Section 19.2: WebAssembly and Rails

WebAssembly, often abbreviated as Wasm, is a binary instruction format designed for web browsers. It allows high-performance execution of code in web browsers and can significantly enhance the capabilities of web applications. In this section, we'll explore how WebAssembly can be integrated with Ruby on Rails and its potential applications.

What is WebAssembly?

WebAssembly is a low-level, binary format that runs at near-native speed in web browsers. Unlike JavaScript, which is a high-level, text-based language, WebAssembly code is compiled to a binary format that is executed directly by the browser. This results in faster load times and improved performance for web applications.

Using WebAssembly in Rails

Integrating WebAssembly with Ruby on Rails can open up various possibilities, such as:

1. **High-Performance Computing**: WebAssembly can be used to run computationally intensive tasks in the browser, such as scientific simulations or 3D rendering.

2. **Enhanced User Interfaces**: You can build complex user interfaces with smooth animations and interactions, leveraging the performance benefits of WebAssembly.

3. **Porting Existing Code**: If you have existing C, C++, or Rust code, you can compile it to WebAssembly and reuse it in your Rails application.

4. **Games and Multimedia**: WebAssembly is well-suited for building web-based games and multimedia applications that require real-time processing.

To get started with WebAssembly in Rails, you can use tools like Emscripten, which is a popular compiler for C and C++ code to WebAssembly. Additionally, you'll need to set up the necessary build pipeline to integrate WebAssembly modules into your Rails application.

Here's a simplified example of how you might use WebAssembly in a Rails application:

```
# Gemfile
gem 'wasm_execjs'

# Install the gem
bundle install

// app/javascript/packs/webassembly.js
import 'wasm_execjs'

const go = new Go();
WebAssembly.instantiateStreaming(fetch('/path/to/your_module.wasm'), go.impor
tObject).then((result) => {
  go.run(result.instance);
});
```

In this example, we import the `wasm_execjs` gem to facilitate running WebAssembly modules in a Rails environment. We then instantiate the WebAssembly module and execute it.

Potential Use Cases

The use cases for WebAssembly in Rails applications are diverse:

- **Data Visualization**: Build interactive data visualization components that handle large datasets with ease.

- **Real-Time Collaboration**: Implement collaborative features with real-time synchronization using WebAssembly for processing changes.

- **Augmented Reality**: Develop web-based augmented reality experiences that run smoothly in the browser.

- **Mathematical Modeling**: Solve complex mathematical problems or perform simulations directly in the browser.

Keep in mind that while WebAssembly brings performance benefits, it's essential to consider the increased complexity it introduces to your application. Proper testing, profiling, and optimization are crucial when working with WebAssembly to ensure a seamless user experience.

Section 19.3: Progressive Web Apps (PWAs)

Progressive Web Apps (PWAs) represent a modern approach to web development that aims to combine the best of both web and mobile app experiences. In this section, we'll delve into what PWAs are, their benefits, and how you can implement them in Ruby on Rails.

What are Progressive Web Apps?

Progressive Web Apps are web applications that offer a native app-like experience to users while being delivered through the web. They are built using standard web technologies (HTML, CSS, JavaScript) but come with several features that make them stand out:

1. **Offline Support**: PWAs can work offline or in low-network conditions, thanks to service workers that cache resources.

2. **Responsive Design**: They provide a consistent experience across various devices and screen sizes.

3. **App-Like Interactions**: PWAs offer smooth animations, gestures, and transitions similar to native apps.

4. **Installable**: Users can add PWAs to their home screens, making them easily accessible like native apps.

5. **Push Notifications**: PWAs can send push notifications to engage users even when the app is not open.

6. **Improved Performance**: They load quickly and respond swiftly to user interactions, enhancing user satisfaction.

Building PWAs with Ruby on Rails

To turn your Ruby on Rails application into a Progressive Web App, you'll need to implement certain features:

1. **Service Workers**: Service workers are JavaScript files that run in the background, intercepting network requests and enabling offline functionality. You can use tools like Workbox to simplify the creation of service workers in Rails.

2. **Web App Manifest**: A manifest file (usually `manifest.json`) describes your app, including its name, icons, and display options. It's used when users install your PWA on their devices.

3. **HTTPS**: PWAs require a secure HTTPS connection to ensure the safety and integrity of data.

Here's a simplified example of how to create a basic service worker in a Rails application:

```javascript
// app/assets/javascripts/service-worker.js

self.addEventListener('install', (event) => {
  event.waitUntil(
    caches.open('my-cache').then((cache) => {
      return cache.addAll([
        '/',
        '/stylesheets/application.css',
        '/images/icon.png',
        // Add more assets to cache as needed
      ]);
    })
  );
});

self.addEventListener('fetch', (event) => {
  event.respondWith(
    caches.match(event.request).then((response) => {
      return response || fetch(event.request);
    })
  );
});
```

In this example, the service worker caches important assets to provide offline support.
You'll also need to register this service worker in your Rails application.

Benefits of PWAs

Progressive Web Apps offer several advantages:

- **Improved User Engagement**: PWAs provide a seamless user experience, leading to higher engagement and retention rates.

- **Cost-Effective**: Developing a PWA is often more cost-effective than building separate native apps for different platforms.

- **Increased Visibility**: PWAs can be discovered through search engines, increasing your app's visibility to potential users.

- **Faster Load Times**: PWAs load quickly, reducing bounce rates and keeping users engaged.

- **Cross-Platform**: A single PWA can work on multiple platforms and devices, eliminating the need for platform-specific development.

- **Easier Maintenance**: Maintaining a single codebase for your PWA simplifies updates and bug fixes.

Considerations

While PWAs offer numerous benefits, they may not be suitable for all types of applications. Consider factors like your target audience, app complexity, and the need for device-specific features when deciding whether to build a PWA.

In summary, Progressive Web Apps provide a compelling approach to delivering high-quality web experiences with the added advantages of offline support, installability, and improved performance. Integrating these features into your Ruby on Rails application can enhance user engagement and satisfaction.

Section 19.4: Serverless Architecture with Rails

In this section, we'll explore the concept of serverless architecture and how you can leverage it in conjunction with your Ruby on Rails application. Serverless computing represents a paradigm shift in how applications are developed, deployed, and scaled.

Understanding Serverless Architecture

Serverless architecture, often referred to as Function as a Service (FaaS), is an approach where developers focus solely on writing code functions while leaving the infrastructure management to a cloud provider like AWS Lambda, Azure Functions, or Google Cloud Functions. Key characteristics of serverless architecture include:

1. **Event-Driven**: Serverless functions are triggered by events, such as HTTP requests, database changes, or scheduled tasks.

2. **Auto-Scaling**: The cloud provider automatically manages the scaling of functions based on incoming requests.

3. **Pay-Per-Use**: You're billed only for the compute resources consumed during the execution of functions, making it cost-effective.

4. **No Server Maintenance**: Developers don't need to worry about server provisioning, patching, or maintenance.

Integrating Serverless with Ruby on Rails

While Ruby on Rails is typically associated with traditional server-based applications, you can integrate serverless components for specific use cases or to offload tasks that benefit from serverless characteristics.

Use Cases for Serverless in Rails:
1. **Background Jobs**: Instead of running background jobs on your Rails server, you can offload them to serverless functions, ensuring scalability and cost-efficiency.

2. **Microservices**: Certain microservices within your Rails application can be implemented as serverless functions, allowing for independent scaling and management.

3. **Image Processing**: Serverless functions can be used to process and optimize images on-the-fly, triggered by user uploads.

4. **Webhooks**: Handling webhooks from external services can be done through serverless functions, ensuring reliability and scalability.

Example of a Serverless Function in Ruby

Here's a simplified example of a serverless function written in Ruby using AWS Lambda and the Serverless Framework:

```yaml
# serverless.yml

service: my-serverless-service

provider:
  name: aws
  runtime: ruby2.7

functions:
  hello:
    handler: handler.hello
```

```ruby
# handler.rb

def hello(event:, context:)
  {
    statusCode: 200,
    body: JSON.generate('message' => 'Hello, Serverless!')
  }
end
```

In this example, the `hello` function responds to HTTP requests with a "Hello, Serverless!" message. This function can be triggered by an API Gateway event, making it accessible via HTTP.

Benefits of Serverless with Rails

Integrating serverless architecture into your Ruby on Rails application can provide several benefits:

- **Cost Savings**: Serverless functions are billed based on usage, reducing infrastructure costs during idle times.

- **Scalability**: Serverless platforms handle automatic scaling, ensuring your application can handle varying workloads.

- **Simplified Deployment**: Deploying serverless functions is typically easier and faster than managing traditional server deployments.

- **Reduced Operational Overhead**: Offloading tasks to serverless reduces the operational burden on your Rails servers.

However, it's essential to carefully consider the trade-offs and suitability of serverless for specific components of your Rails application. Not all use cases benefit from this architecture, so thoughtful design and planning are crucial. Serverless can complement your Rails application, providing flexibility and cost-efficiency where needed.

Section 19.5: Exploring AI and Machine Learning in Rails Apps

In this section, we'll delve into the exciting realm of artificial intelligence (AI) and machine learning (ML) and discuss how you can integrate these technologies into your Ruby on Rails applications. AI and ML have gained significant prominence in recent years, and their applications in web development are both diverse and powerful.

AI and ML in Web Development

AI and ML offer a wide range of capabilities that can enhance your Rails applications:

1. **Recommendation Systems**: Implement personalized content recommendations for users based on their behavior and preferences. This can be invaluable for e-commerce platforms, content-driven websites, and more.

2. **Predictive Analytics**: Use machine learning models to predict future trends, user behavior, or system performance. For instance, predicting user churn can help in customer retention strategies.

3. **Natural Language Processing (NLP)**: Leverage NLP models to analyze and understand text data. This can be used for sentiment analysis, chatbots, and content summarization.

4. **Computer Vision**: Incorporate computer vision algorithms to process and interpret images and videos. This can be applied in image recognition, object detection, and augmented reality features.

5. **Anomaly Detection**: Detect unusual patterns or anomalies in data, which is crucial for fraud detection, system monitoring, and security applications.

Integrating AI/ML in Rails

To integrate AI and ML into your Ruby on Rails application, consider the following steps:

1. **Data Collection and Preparation**: Gather relevant data for training and testing your models. This could be user behavior data, text, images, or any other relevant information. Ensure the data is clean and well-structured.

2. **Model Development**: Develop machine learning models using libraries like TensorFlow, PyTorch, or scikit-learn for Python. These models can be trained to perform various tasks such as classification, regression, clustering, and more.

3. **API Integration**: Expose your AI/ML models through APIs that your Rails application can communicate with. You can use RESTful API endpoints or GraphQL for this purpose.

4. **Front-End Integration**: Implement the necessary user interfaces and components to interact with AI-driven features. This could involve displaying recommendations, chatbots, or visualizing data from ML predictions.

Example of AI/ML Integration

Let's consider an example of integrating a recommendation system into a Rails e-commerce application:

```ruby
# app/controllers/products_controller.rb

class ProductsController < ApplicationController
  def show
    @product = Product.find(params[:id])

    # Call the recommendation system API to fetch related products
    response = HTTP.get("https://recommendation-api.example.com/recommend?product_id=#{params[:id]}")
    @related_products = JSON.parse(response.body)
  end
end
```

In this example, when a user views a product, the Rails controller calls an external recommendation system API to fetch related products based on the current product. These related products are then displayed to the user.

Benefits of AI/ML in Rails

The integration of AI and ML into your Rails application can provide several advantages:

- **Personalization**: Enhance user experience by providing personalized content and recommendations.

- **Efficiency**: Automate tasks and processes, reducing manual effort and improving efficiency.

- **Insights**: Gain insights from data analysis that can drive business decisions and strategies.

- **Competitive Advantage**: Stay ahead of the competition by offering innovative features and services.

However, it's essential to consider the ethical and privacy implications of AI and ML in your application, especially when handling sensitive user data. Additionally, machine learning models require continuous monitoring and updates to maintain their accuracy and relevance. Proper testing and evaluation are also critical to ensure the models perform as expected.

In conclusion, AI and ML can add significant value to your Ruby on Rails applications, opening up new possibilities for user engagement, data analysis, and automation. By carefully planning and integrating these technologies, you can stay at the forefront of web development trends and provide cutting-edge solutions to your users.

Chapter 20: Conclusion and Next Steps

Section 20.1: Reflecting on Your Journey

As we come to the conclusion of this comprehensive guide to Ruby on Rails, it's essential to take a moment to reflect on your journey as a Rails developer. You've embarked on a path filled with learning, challenges, and growth, and it's worth acknowledging your accomplishments and the knowledge you've gained.

Celebrating Your Achievements

Throughout this book, you've explored a wide range of topics related to Ruby on Rails, from the fundamentals of the framework to advanced techniques and best practices. You've built web applications, learned how to work with databases, mastered controllers and views, and even dabbled in topics like testing, security, and AI integration.

Take a moment to celebrate your achievements. Think about the projects you've completed, the problems you've solved, and the skills you've acquired. Each chapter you've completed represents a milestone in your Rails journey.

Setting Future Goals

As a developer, the learning journey never truly ends. Technology evolves rapidly, and there are always new tools, frameworks, and best practices to explore. Consider setting future goals to continue your growth as a Rails developer:

1. **Advanced Topics**: Dive deeper into specific areas that interest you the most. This could be mastering front-end frameworks like React or exploring advanced database optimization techniques.

2. **Contribution to Open Source**: Contribute to open source Rails projects. It's an excellent way to give back to the community and gain valuable experience.

3. **Certifications**: Consider pursuing relevant certifications to validate your skills. For example, you could aim for Ruby on Rails certification or AWS certification if you're working with cloud services.

4. **Entrepreneurship**: If you have innovative ideas, think about building your startup using Rails. Many successful startups began with a small team and a Rails application.

5. **Mentorship**: Share your knowledge and mentor aspiring developers. Teaching can deepen your understanding and benefit others.

Embracing Lifelong Learning

Remember that software development is a field that requires continuous learning. New technologies, programming languages, and methodologies emerge regularly. Embrace the concept of lifelong learning, where you consistently seek out new knowledge and adapt to industry changes.

Joining developer communities, attending conferences, reading tech blogs, and participating in online courses are excellent ways to stay updated. Don't hesitate to explore areas outside of Rails as well; a broad skill set can make you a more versatile developer.

Final Thoughts

We've covered a vast array of topics in this book, equipping you with the skills and knowledge needed to create robust and innovative Ruby on Rails applications. Whether you're pursuing a career as a Rails developer, building side projects, or working on your startup, Rails provides a powerful framework to bring your ideas to life.

Your Rails journey is an ongoing adventure, and there's no limit to what you can achieve. Stay curious, keep coding, and continue building amazing web applications. Your future in web development is bright, and you have the tools to shape it in exciting ways.

Thank you for joining us on this Rails exploration. Best of luck with your coding endeavors, and may your Rails applications be both elegant and functional.

Section 20.2: Setting Future Goals as a Rails Developer

Now that you've reached the conclusion of this book and are equipped with a solid foundation in Ruby on Rails, it's time to look ahead and set future goals for your journey as a Rails developer.

1. Advanced Specialization

Consider specializing in a particular area within Ruby on Rails. Whether it's front-end development, back-end optimization, or mobile app integration, specialization can make you a sought-after expert in a specific niche.

2. Contributions to Open Source

Open source contributions are a valuable way to enhance your skills and give back to the developer community. Look for Rails-related open source projects that align with your interests and expertise. Becoming a contributor can help you gain recognition and experience.

3. Continuous Learning

The tech industry evolves rapidly. Stay updated with the latest developments in Ruby on Rails and related technologies. Attend conferences, participate in webinars, and subscribe to newsletters and blogs that cover Ruby on Rails news and trends.

4. Certifications

Consider pursuing certifications in Ruby on Rails or related technologies. Certifications can validate your expertise and make you stand out in the job market.

5. Entrepreneurship

If you have innovative ideas, think about building your own startup using Ruby on Rails. Many successful companies, including GitHub and Airbnb, began as startups built on this framework.

6. Mentorship and Teaching

Share your knowledge with others by becoming a mentor or instructor. Teaching can deepen your understanding of Ruby on Rails and contribute to the growth of the developer community.

7. Networking

Networking is essential in the tech industry. Attend meetups, conferences, and online forums to connect with fellow developers, potential collaborators, and job opportunities.

8. Diversity in Your Portfolio

Expand your portfolio by working on diverse projects. Consider building web applications for different industries, such as e-commerce, healthcare, or finance, to broaden your skill set.

9. Remote Work and Freelancing

Explore remote work opportunities or freelance gigs. Remote work allows you to work with clients and teams from around the world, providing unique experiences and the flexibility to manage your schedule.

10. Contribution to the Ruby on Rails Community

Get involved in the Ruby on Rails community. You can participate in discussions, help answer questions on forums, and contribute to Rails documentation. Your contributions can have a positive impact on the community and help you build a reputation as an active member.

Remember that setting goals is just the beginning. It's essential to break them down into smaller, actionable steps and consistently work toward them. As you continue your journey as a Rails developer, stay curious, stay passionate, and never stop learning. The tech world is full of opportunities, and your skills in Ruby on Rails can open many doors.

Section 20.3: Resources for Advanced Learning

As you conclude this book and embark on your journey as a seasoned Ruby on Rails developer, it's essential to have access to advanced learning resources that can help you stay at the forefront of Rails development and related technologies. This section provides a curated list of resources to further your knowledge and skills.

1. Advanced Rails Books

- **"Advanced Rails"** by Brad Ediger: This book dives deep into advanced Rails topics, including testing, performance optimization, and security.
- **"Metaprogramming Ruby 2"** by Paolo Perrotta: Understanding metaprogramming in Ruby is essential for advanced Rails development.

2. Rails Blogs and Newsletters

- Ruby on Rails Blog: The official Ruby on Rails blog provides updates, news, and announcements from the Rails core team.
- Ruby Weekly: A weekly newsletter featuring the latest news, articles, and gems related to Ruby and Rails.

3. Online Courses and Tutorials

- RailsCasts: A collection of short screencasts covering advanced Rails topics.
- Pluralsight: Offers a wide range of courses on Rails, including advanced topics.

4. Advanced Ruby and Rails Podcasts

- The Ruby on Rails Podcast: Features interviews with Rails experts and discussions on advanced Rails topics.

5. Advanced Ruby and Rails Conferences

- RailsConf: An annual conference dedicated to Ruby on Rails, featuring advanced talks and workshops.
- RubyConf: The annual Ruby conference often includes advanced Ruby and Rails content.

6. Advanced Ruby Gems

- Pry: A powerful runtime developer console and IRB alternative for Ruby.
- Sidekiq: A popular background processing framework for Ruby that can handle advanced queuing and job processing.

7. Advanced Testing Tools

- RSpec: An advanced testing framework for Ruby, commonly used in Rails applications.
- Capybara: An acceptance test framework for web applications, often used for Rails integration testing.

8. Advanced Deployment and DevOps

- **Docker**: Learn containerization to simplify Rails application deployment.
- **Kubernetes**: Explore Kubernetes for container orchestration in advanced Rails deployment scenarios.

9. Contributing to Open Source

- **Ruby on Rails GitHub Repository**: Contribute to the Rails framework itself, and gain experience by working on issues and pull requests.

10. Advanced Meetups and Communities

- Join local Rails meetups or online communities like **[Stack Overflow](https://stackoverflow.com/questions/tagged/ruby-on-rails)** to engage with experienced Rails developers.

Remember that advanced learning is a continuous journey. Be proactive in seeking out new challenges, experimenting with cutting-edge technologies, and sharing your knowledge with the community. By staying committed to lifelong learning, you can excel as a Ruby on Rails developer and contribute to the ever-evolving world of web development.

Section 20.4: Final Thoughts and Farewell

Congratulations on reaching the end of this comprehensive guide to Ruby on Rails! As you reflect on your journey through these chapters, it's important to take a moment for some final thoughts and considerations.

Reflecting on Your Progress

Think back to when you started this book. You may have been a beginner in Ruby on Rails, or perhaps you had some prior experience. Regardless of your starting point, you've come a long way. You've learned about the fundamentals of Rails, built applications, mastered controllers and views, explored testing, and delved into advanced topics. Take pride in your accomplishments.

The Ongoing Learning Process

Remember that software development is a field of constant growth and change. New technologies emerge, best practices evolve, and the web development landscape continues to shift. Embrace the fact that learning is a lifelong journey. Stay curious, stay engaged, and stay eager to learn.

Setting Future Goals

With your newfound skills and knowledge, you're now equipped to set ambitious goals for your career as a Rails developer. Consider your next steps. Is there a specific type of project you want to work on? Are there areas within Rails that you want to specialize in, such as API development, performance optimization, or security? Setting clear goals can guide your path forward.

Contributing to the Community

Open source communities thrive because of contributions from developers like you. Consider giving back to the Rails community by contributing to the framework itself, sharing your knowledge through blog posts or tutorials, or helping newcomers in forums and discussion groups. Your contributions can make a meaningful impact.

Staying Inspired

Staying inspired is crucial for your long-term success. Attend conferences, meetups, and webinars to connect with other developers and stay updated on industry trends. Read books, blogs, and articles to gain fresh perspectives. Keep experimenting with side projects to nurture your creativity.

Farewell and Thank You

As you close this book, know that this is not the end of your journey but the beginning of an exciting career in Ruby on Rails development. I want to express my gratitude for choosing this guide as a part of your learning journey. Thank you for your dedication and hard work.

Wishing you all the best in your future endeavors as a Ruby on Rails developer. Farewell, and may your code always run smoothly and your web applications shine brightly in the digital world!

Section 20.5: Acknowledgments and Credits

As we conclude this book, it's important to acknowledge the contributions and efforts of the many individuals and organizations that have made this resource possible. Writing a comprehensive guide like this involves the collective wisdom and support of a community. Here, we express our gratitude and provide credits to those who have played a significant role in shaping this book.

Contributors

This guide wouldn't be complete without the contributions of various developers and experts who shared their knowledge, code examples, and real-world experiences. While it's not possible to list everyone individually, we extend our gratitude to the Ruby on Rails community at large.

Open Source Projects

Many open source projects and libraries have been referenced and utilized throughout this book. These projects have significantly contributed to the Rails ecosystem, and we encourage readers to explore and support them.

Publishing Team

Behind the scenes, there's a dedicated team that has worked on editing, formatting, and publishing this book. Their efforts have played a crucial role in making this guide accessible to readers.

Special Thanks

We would like to express our gratitude to the creators and maintainers of Ruby on Rails, as well as the Ruby programming language. Their visionary work has shaped the world of web development and provided us with powerful tools.

Your Support

Last but not least, we want to thank you, the reader, for choosing to embark on this learning journey with us. Your support and engagement are what make projects like this worthwhile.

As we wrap up this book, we hope you continue your exploration of Ruby on Rails and the broader field of web development. Your curiosity, dedication, and passion for coding will undoubtedly lead you to exciting opportunities and new horizons.